OUTSTANDING YOUTH!

# OUTSTANDING YOUTH!

## A NOVEL

COOPER RUMRILL

NEW DEGREE PRESS

COPYRIGHT © 2020 COOPER RUMRILL

OUTSTANDING YOUTH!
*A Novel*

| ISBN | | |
|------|---------------------|----------------|
| | 978-1-63676-529-7 | *Paperback* |
| | 978-1-63676-069-8 | *Kindle Ebook* |
| | 978-1-63676-070-4 | *Ebook* |

*Mom, this one's for you.*
*I apologize in advance.*

# CONTENTS

———

# AUTHOR'S NOTE

———

*Freaks and Geeks. Pretty Little Liars. Gossip Girl. Friday Night Lights. Glee. Riverdale. Sex Education. On My Block. 13 Reasons Why. Euphoria.* High school television, ranging from cutesy to kitschy, sincere to serious, to whatever the hell you want to call *Glee.* But the average age of the shows' creators/developers? Thirty-nine.

Why is it that all high school shows are made by people who haven't opened a high school locker in over twenty years?

A large part of the reason why the average age of a high school television show's creator is nearly forty is because creating a TV show is a risk to a Hollywood studio, and Hollywood values experience. This argument falls a bit flat when you consider this: the average age of the creators and developers for ten of the most popular shows about twenty-somethings (*Friends, Sex and the City, How I Met Your Mother, New Girl, Community, Girls, Don't Trust the B**** in Apartment 23, The Mindy Show, 2 Broke Girls, and Atlanta*) is a spry young thirty-two and a half. Most depictions of life as a twenty-something on the silver screen are curated from the minds of people immediately removed from their twenties. Most depictions of high school on the silver screen are curated from the minds of people who've had twenty years to soak their memories of high school in a vat of nostalgia.

Everyone remembers their Prom, but what thirty-nine-year-old remembers the day before Prom? Or the day before that?

Nostalgia polarizes memories. The good times were *great*. The bad times were *awful*. And maybe they were. If you've got a mortgage, a receding hairline, two bratty kids who won't shut up, and in-laws who drive you up a wall, it's easy to remember high school as *the good old days*. You don't remember how absolutely crushed you were over the petty bullshit, or how overwhelmed you were with schoolwork and college and this and that. You don't remember what you laughed about, just that you laughed. A lot.

You can't make a compelling TV show solely based off of an aestheticized memory, though. You've got to add drama. Only problem is, you're limited to your five or six central characters. So you've gotta pump about five or six metric tons of high school drama into the lives of your poor protagonists (or in the case of *13 Reasons Why*, thirteen metric tons of capital-D *Drama,* and slap a Content Warning with a *"Fuck You, It's Educational"* in the title card before each episode for good measure). If your show gets approved for another season, the characters must endure another season of stereotypically *serious* high school problems.

High school movies are a bit more sensible. Consider these classics and modern triumphs: *The Breakfast Club, Ferris Bueller's Day Off, Fast Times at Ridgemont High, Dazed and Confused,*

*Mean Girls, Superbad, Easy A, Lady Bird, Booksmart,* and *The Edge of Seventeen.* The average age of the screenwriter for these movies is twenty-nine—ten years younger than the high school niche's television counterpart. These writers were, on average, only eleven years removed from their own high school days.

At twenty-one years old, I've only recently been able to conceive what eleven years feels like. I remember being ten years old in third grade. Mrs. Fox's classroom. My buddies Andrew and David. Recess. Would I now feel confident writing a book about elementary school? Absolutely not. Is that a faulty analogy? It definitely is. Is that even an analogy? Probably not.

When the media we consume purports to clue us in as to what high school life is *actually* like, we believe it. I know what it was like to be a high schooler in the eighties despite being born in 1999. Same goes for anything we see on a screen, really. I know what it was like to be in the mob in the fifties. I know what it's like to peddle drugs in New Mexico. I know what the zombie apocalypse is like. I've seen it.

I understand why actual mobsters, meth dealers, and zombie-apocalypse survivors don't write Hollywood scripts about their Honest-to-God trials and tribulations. These are professions that Hollywood has glorified because they're so far removed from our typical hum-drum. But doesn't Hollywood glorify high school to the same extent? For adults, high school is youth. For middle-schoolers, high school is freedom. For high schoolers, high school is...?

Seth Rogan and Evan Goldberg began writing *Superbad* in earnest when they were eighteen, and it shows. That movie is timeless. It doesn't matter that it came out in 2007, its portrayal of high school students transcends the flip phones, the 2000s fashion, the Michael Cera. The characters are real, their motivations and their interactions with each other are real, too. Compare that to the excess and nostalgic revision of *Ferris Bueller's Day Off*, written by a thirty-nine-year-old John Hughes fresh off of the success of his prior movie, *The Breakfast Club*. Don't get me wrong, *Ferris* is a wonderful movie. Is it *really* a high school movie, though?

Ferris is a literal daydream of confidence and coolness, Ed Rooney is a caricature of Wile-E-Coyote, Sloane is a supermodel. Cameron, presented as eighteen, is played by a twenty-nine-year-old. It's as much a high school movie as *South Park* is a show about middle-schoolers.

*Ferris Bueller's Day Off* still kicks a lot of ass, obviously. I just can't help but get the feeling that John Hughes had a wet dream about himself twenty years earlier—standing up to a bully and asking his crush out on a date, while simultaneously being Paul McCartney circa 1964—and decided to write a screenplay about it.

So here's me, at twenty-one, trying to remember the (metaphorical, I swear) wet dreams I had when I was actually *in* high school, and reconcile their relationship to whatever the hell was actually going on in my life and the lives of my friends. That came out wrong. Pun intended.

What I mean to say is that I'm trying to remember what it was like to *be* a high schooler before I overly sentimentalize the experience. Maybe it's too late, who knows. I guess it's impossible to have absolute faith in your memory.

A bit about my high school experience: I went to a co-ed boarding school (400 students) in New England whose dress code was Vineyard Vines quarter zips with salmon shorts. Our mascot was a zebra, I shit you not. Most of the students were always stressed about schoolwork. Nearly half of us played on some varsity team. Everybody went to college. I lived in a dorm.

So that's what I've written about here. St. Dominic's isn't my high school, Mark and Birdie and the other characters aren't my friends, and the shit that goes down in the book (mostly) never actually happened, not to me or my friends at least. But maybe it is, maybe they are, and maybe it did.

The story here is told all out of order, a sequence of vignettes scrambled over the course of a year (September 2018 to August 2019). If I were bold I'd call it a kaleidoscopic map of youth; in my humility I'll admit I just didn't know any other way to tell this story.

One of the most profound conversations I've ever had was with a good friend of mine during a long drive up North. We discussed whether or not profundity itself is objective or subjective. I don't remember the conclusions we reached or the arguments we made, but the sentiments of that conversation still echo around in my brain from time to time. What is a profound text? A profound experience? Is something profound itself, or is it just profound to you?

///*Life moves pretty fast...*///

# ONE

# (THE FIRST FRIDAY OF SUMMER)

———

Maud confirmed her little brother's count: "We've only got fifty cards."

"So we're missing two?"

"Which two?"

"Give me half the deck, sort them into suits."

They sorted the deck into suits.

"Now, give me the reds, I'll give you the blacks."

Maud gave him the reds, Birdie gave her the blacks.

"We don't have the Six of Diamonds," said Birdie.

"Or the Jack of Spades," Maud concluded, smacking a mosquito on her thigh. "What are we going to do?"

"Let me think." Birdie got off of the sofa and moseyed toward the kitchenette.

"I've got it," said Birdie after grabbing a lite beer from the fridge. "Take out all the Aces."

"Okay, I've taken the Aces out," Maud said. "Can you toss me a beer?"

Birdie tossed her a beer, then sat back down on the sofa. Maud sat across from him in a pastel blue wingback chair. The cards lay face-up and organized on the coffee table between the two siblings. Birdie took hold of the Ace of Diamonds and the Ace of Spades. "Alright, look: this is now the Six of Diamonds."

"And that's the Jack of Spades?" Maud pointed and understood.

"Yep."

"So no Aces?"

"Nope."

That's how they got around having only fifty cards: by playing with forty-eight. The game was Gin Rummy. Maud melded four times before Birdie could scrape together a 5-A-7 Diamond straight. Maud put down three Jacks, and Birdie added an Eight to his straight.

"You know, I never understood the story of how this house burned down," Birdie said after discarding the Four of Clubs.

"That's because Grandpa tells it differently every time." Maud, realizing she had been holding onto the Ace of Spades, placed it down on top of her three Jacks to win the game.

They were in the new guest house. The old guest house had been built at the same time as Fayter Cottage in 1898, but burnt down in 1948 after Albert Fayter Jr.—son of the first Albert Fayter , father of Albert Fayter Sr., and grandfather to Birdie and Maud Fayter—accidentally placed an insecticide spray-can in the burn pile of trash out back by the shed behind the guest house. That 3rd of July, young Albert, sixteen at the time, was drinking Vat 69 (which he had smuggled from the bottom shelf of his father's whiskey cabinet) straight from the bottle with several of his mates who also summered at Sippewissett, when suddenly a mosquito hissed into his ear. In reflex, Albert swung at the insect, Vat 69 in hand. The bottle luckily did not break, though it crashed against his ear with enough velocity to give him permanent hearing damage.

Immediately hard of hearing, throbbing with pain, and drunk as all fuck, Albert took out the DDT insecticide from the tall, skinny closet by the back door and sprayed the entire interior of the guest house's first floor to exterminate any lingering mosquitoes. He could not hear his friends telling him to stop, he only saw them running out of the house coughing and rubbing at their eyes. When the can ran dry, Albert threw it into the burn pile out back and fell asleep in the yard, face down and ass up.

He was awoken the next day by Bomber, the family's white and buff cocker spaniel, licking his nose. Ronnie, the housekeeper, burnt the trash that day at three o'clock in the afternoon. The trash, the shed, and the guest house burnt down shortly after in a fiery kaboom. Ronnie, gimpy from a lingering cartilage tear in his knee, walked unwittingly (in what one might call slow-motion) straight into the explosion and unfortunately perished.

The Fayter family couldn't bear not having a guest house, nor a housekeeper, nor a shed, so they rebuilt the guest house and the shed the following year in the trendy colonial Cape Cod style of the mid-twentieth century. Ronnie, may he rest in pieces, was soon replaced by Carmine. Carmine would keep the house for fifty years, until his own death in 2000. Carmine's son Ronaldo kept the house in the twenty years since. Ronaldo's son, coincidentally also named Ronnie, planned on inheriting the full labor of the house once his father retired to Boca Raton in 2028.

Though constructed over seventy years ago, the guest house had remained affectionately titled "The New Guest House."

Sometimes it was the Vat 69 their grandfather and his pals had been drinking, other times it was the Park & Tilford Reserve bottle. Sometimes he had stolen it from his father's whiskey cabinet, other times from Sturgill's General Store of Brewster. Sometimes Sturgill's General Store "of Brewster" was actually "of Hyannis." Sometimes Albert Fayter Jr., or just Junior, insisted whiskey with an 'e' came from Scotland, and sometimes everywhere *but* Scotland.

The major differences between the many iterations of the story often began and ended with a discussion of the merits and demerits of vintage whiskeys. The major plot points of the mosquito and the insecticide and the permanent hearing loss and Bomber and Ronnie remained, for the most part, unchanged (and accompanied by the same dramatic gestures and reenactments). Although they always got a good laugh, those gestures and reenactments were becoming scarcer and scarcer in Junior's storytelling (Junior being their grandfather), as he could no longer get out of his chair or flail his arms with the dramatic urgency required for the visual gag in his older age.

Birdie counted his deadwood cards. "Grandpa only tells the story differently," he began, "because he's tired of telling the same story all the time." He got up to get another beer.

Maud burped and threw her empty can at her younger brother. "So what don't you understand about the story?" she asked as she turned herself over to lean over the backside of the couch, facing the kitchenette.

Birdie stood on the tiled quarter of the floor, opened his beer, and watched the foam fizz up and over the can, down his hand, and onto the floor.

"It doesn't matter," he said. "Want to play again?"

Maud shrugged, then flipped back to sitting regularly on the couch. She shimmied her phone out of the back pocket of her skinny blue jeans.

Birdie mumbled something like "'ma take apiss" and shut the bathroom door behind him with more force than intended.

Maud looked over her shoulder to make sure he was in fact behind a closed door then quickly withdrew her Juul from her bra and took several deep, quick rips. She did her best to exhale down her blouse by curling her lower lip around her bottom teeth, although some of the vapor trickled and drifted awkwardly outward. She swatted at the vapor and broke it up with her hand, which tightly gripped the yellow smiley pop socket on her phone. Her Juul had several small plastic jewels bedazzling its sleek metal frame.

Maisie O'Connor, one of Maud's roommates at St. Dominic's Preparatory Academy, referred to the Juul as a 'jewel Juul,' a nickname which was eventually abridged to 'JuJu' by Maud's other friends. Inquiries such as "Mind if I kiss JuJu?" or "Is JuJu ready to play?" or "Hey, let me see JuJu!" were cheeky ways for Maud's friends to see if they could use the Juul.

Maud thought that Birdie had been in the bathroom for far too long for a regular piss, so must be in fact shitting. She figured she had at least another minute or so, and practiced blowing O's.

In the bathroom, Birdie also took out his Juul and covertly ripped it with long steady inhales and quick exhales. He sat on the toilet lid and took several rips before fearing Maud would notice the unexpected silence of his trip to the bathroom. He stood and tried his best to splash out some urine (all the while ripping his Juul sans hands, puffing out vapor on either side of the vape held in the center of his mouth with his teeth). Unfortunately for Birdie, the well was quite dry. He thought about turning on the faucet at a low-pressure trickle, but figured the sound would be too distant from that of a beer-induced piss break.

Birdie instead slowly poured out his Whale's Tale Pale Ale into the toilet, satisfied that the sound emulated that of a steady stream of beer-piss. He realized then (about twenty seconds after Maud) that he had been in the bathroom for an awkward duration, one between a long piss and a quick shit, and decided he could afford another minute or so of continuous nicotine consumption.

Unlike Maud's, Birdie's Juul didn't have a specific moniker his friends could address when they needed their nic fix. Instead, it was customary for them to refer to the vape as any celebrity or shared acquaintance's name that began with the letter 'J.' "Could I see Julio Jones?" or "Can I get a rip of Justin Timberlake?" or (and this one was a bit of a stretch, but nevertheless got a laugh) "Can I chief the DiGiorno?"

Birdie took one last look at the light brown ale-water fizzing in the toilet before flushing it down. He turned on the sink to buy himself another ten seconds for one last rip then emerged back into the living room/kitchenette, wiping his dry hands on his sweatpants.

"Who's coming tonight?" Maud asked as Birdie sat back down.

"A bunch of people."

"Let me guess…Mark?"

"Yes, my dear roommate Mark will be joining us this evening."

"His girlfriend?"

"Ex-girlfriend these days. Grace. Yeah, she's coming."

"Oof."

"Oof indeed," Birdie concurred.

"Okay, who else? Todd and Frank?"

"Those clowns, yeah. Chris, too."

"I always get Todd and Frank mixed up."

"Fraud and Tank, as they say."

"Who says that?"

"Maury used to say that. His little sister's coming tonight too."

"Carissa Moraine?"

"Yep. And her roommate Sarah—"

"You invited a *Moraine* to our house?"

Birdie threw a pillow at his sister. "Don't be like that," he said.

Maud laughed. "Only teasing. She's a sweet girl."

"Yeah, she really is."

"Shame, though."

"Yeah, it really is."

After a stint of silence, Birdie remembered that Jess was coming too, though he didn't feel the need to mention it. Maud announced that the beer was running right through her, and went to the bathroom. So the siblings re-enacted the scene of just a few moments prior, their positions swapped.

/// *They say that one Juul pod contains as much nicotine as a pack of cigarettes. Birdie went through a pod or so a day, while it took Maud several days to finish one. By Birdie's own estimate, after nine months of owning his own Juul, he had purchased seventy-one packs at $22 a pack, amounting to a grand total of $1,562.* ///

# (THE SNOW DAY)

———

It was still dark outside when Mark Duplessis woke up. He didn't awake with a startle as he would from a bad dream, nor did he wake up with an erection as he would from a dream that was frighteningly good. He didn't wake up sweaty, and he didn't wake up cold. He didn't have to piss, nor had he pissed himself. He simply opened his eyes and was awake.

Mark could tell this was the kind of awake he wouldn't be able to go back to sleep from, so he guessed it must be close to sunrise. He eventually took out his phone from underneath his pillow. 6:10 AM.

He had just received a twelve-foot-long charging cable from his Aunt Melinda at Christmas, which finally allowed him to keep his phone with him up on the top bunk at night. This new convenience revolutionized both the manner by which Mark woke in the mornings and the manner by which Mark masturbated at night. No longer did he have to hop out of bed to frantically turn off his alarm so that he didn't wake up Birdie; now he could set his alarm to 'vibrate only' and place it under his pillow.  Moreover, pornography had never before been available after he and Birdie turned off the lights at night (at least not without sacrificing his phone's next-day battery).

On that latter point, Mark did not feel morally disgusted with himself for, on many occasions in the fall when he had trouble falling asleep, soft squeaks and patters had reverberated from the bunk below him. In the two weeks since they'd returned from winter break, Mark would sometimes wait until he was sure Birdie was asleep before taking off one of his socks and reaping the unintended benefits of Auntie Melinda's Christmas present.

That morning Mark quietly hopped out of bed and walked to the bathroom in his underwear and lone sock.

///On two of those nights during which Mark beat his meat, Birdie lay awake horrified, as he too had been waiting until he was sure Mark was asleep. This they never discussed. ///

# (THE FIRST DAY
# OF SCHOOL)

———

It was the first day of junior year at St. Dominic's Preparatory Academy. The air was hot and the windows were open. The construction of the new dormitory on the west side of campus filled the classroom with reverberating bangs and buzzes. Walsh was one of the oldest buildings on campus. Exposed white pipes tracked along the ceiling, interlaced with cobwebs and flakes of rust.

Henry Dinelli aired out his shirt. Mr. McMahon thumbed through his copy of *The Collected Works of Robert Frost* from across the great wooden Harkness table, breathing through his stomach. To McMahon's left sat Devin and Gabe, commuters who were rarely seen on campus outside of class. Then there was Lucy and Stacy and Megan and Maddie, who were chatting about their classes and their summers and their this and their that. Next sat Birdie, digging dirt out from under his nails with the tip of a mechanical pencil, and Frank, who was texting in some meme-sharing, casually misogynistic and homophobic groupchat, probably. Simon O'Malley, who was straightening out his blue folder with his blue notebook and his blue pen all laid neatly out in front of him, sat to McMahon's right. The bell rang and Henry realized that the only two open seats around the table were to his immediate left and his immediate right.

McMahon began roll call alphabetically by last name and, as there were no A's, B's, or C's in the class, Henry Dinelli was first on the list.

"No man is an island," McMahon began after Henry muttered 'here,' "but you certainly seem alone over there." All eyes turned to Henry, who had about a third of the table to himself and his vacant neighboring chairs. "What's the problem, guys? Did Henry forget to wear deodorant this morning?"

Some laughter, especially from Simon. Classic fucking Simon.

"I smell just fine," Henry said with a smile. Play it cool, play it casual.

"Your peers may very well disagree," McMahon said. "Okay, moving on…Duvall?"

*Here.* "Fayter?" *Yup.* "Fink?" *Here.* "Fletcher?" *Here.* "Um, Megan…I'm going to butcher your last name…," *It's Bad-Ah-Mo-See.* "Gbadamosi, got it. Lee?" *Here.* "Li?" *Here.* "Did you guys get that right?" *Chuckles. Yes.* "Moraine?"

Henry's stomach tensed up. His cheeks became tingly.

"Carissa Moraine? No?" People around the tables pursed their lips and raised their eyebrows to indicate *no, she's not here.* "We'll give her another couple of minutes, it being the first day and all."

Frank whispered something to Birdie that made him smile.

Henry's ass suddenly became sweaty. McMahon finished the roll with Simon O'Malley, who said "present" like *pre*-sent.

The teacher scooched his chair in toward the table, laid his elbows down, clasped his hands, sighed, and began, "Well, welcome to...," when in stumbled Carissa, gleaming and glistening and radiant and whole.

"Is this...I'm so sorry...," She asked in between heavy breaths and immediately apologizing.

"You must be Carissa," McMahon said, emulating the tone of voice of some eighties high school movie (whether he intended to or not). "Take a seat, catch your breath. We've barely begun." Carissa went over to the back side of the table and sat between Henry and Birdie. "Be advised, Carissa Moraine. Henry isn't wearing any deodorant."

Henry, who had been examining the word *Ticonderoga* in his syllabus with utmost focus, dropped his pencil onto the table and thought of something to say. Unfortunately, he never said it. He just pursed his lips coyly.

Carissa was wearing a pair of bright green shorts and a tie-dye Grateful Dead t-shirt which she had cut and tied into a crop top. She sat down and pulled out her big blue water bottle and a white notebook. She rummaged through her bag for a minute while McMahon passed out syllabi before whispering to those near her, "*Can I borrow a pen?*"

"Yeah, sure," Birdie answered. He gave her his pen, and she thanked him.

Henry didn't move a muscle. His eyes were still locked onto the syllabus, examining it with the sort of scrutiny that suggested he was looking for some hidden implication or loophole to either point out or exploit. In truth, he was merely looking intently at the word *semester* and trying to hold in a fart.

Birdie and Carissa exchanged, in whispers, brief salutations and recapitulations of their summers.

Once he broke out of his *semester* fixation, Henry flipped through the pages of the syllabus with such feigned consternation as to suggest that he was both an attentive reader and that he didn't plan on listening to much of what Mr. McMahon would be saying that semester. Carissa didn't seem to notice. After Henry had perused the pages on plagiarism and the honor code and weekly quizzes, he found at the bottom of the last page a final paragraph headed *Accessibility, Mental Health, and Alternative Participation.* The section read as follows:

*As a teacher at St. Dominic's Preparatory Academy, I have sworn myself to educate to the best of my ability. In order to do so, I need to be aware of any learning disabilities so as to ensure every student receives an equal pedagogical experience. Furthermore, as 25 percent of your final grade in this class is your participation, I also would like to know if you have any mental health-related concerns which would hinder your ability to actively and vocally participate in class. A student with severe social anxiety, for example, should speak with me to find a way to fairly assess their participation in ways other than in-class contributions (independent writing assignments, private conversations about the text, or graded notetaking are several ways to gauge engagement with the material).*

Henry thought it was strange to read *gauge engage* as his mind focused on anything that wasn't the fact that Carissa fucking Moraine was sitting next to him. She smelled like coconut shampoo. Fuck. Outside a gas-powered cut-off saw screamed as it split a slab of stone in half. Someone coughed.

"And, well I hate to do it," Mr. McMahon said, "but I truly do need you all to be doing the readings. So there will be unannounced pop quizzes every week or so, to ensure you are all doing them."

Birdie and Frank moaned in comic disapproval.

"The readings are important for our discussions. I don't like being the only one during a class who knows what's going on." Mr. McMahon fanned his syllabus toward his face. Deep blue stains of sweat seeped out of the armpits of his light blue dress shirt. "And I've read all the SparkNotes, all the CliffsNotes. The questions on these pop quizzes will have obvious answers to true readers, yet will stump anyone reliant on deviant third-party shortcuts. Any questions so far?"

That jackass Simon O'Malley of course asked what those quizzes would look like, which in all fairness Henry was curious about himself—but under no circumstance would he ever be so eager as to ask his teacher, in front of the class, what would be on a quiz for material they hadn't even covered yet. They would most likely be multiple choice, Henry was glad to hear.

It seemed as if the construction workers outside were just loudly banging shit together for the sake of making noise.

"Alright, so uh, we're gonna do something now I haven't done before," McMahon began. "If everybody could read the next passage here, *Accessibility, Mental Health, and Alternative Participation*…so, when we're done reading that…" After another beat he asked, "Okay, has everyone read the passage?"

Just blank stares and the sound of splitting stones outside.

"Right, then. It's quite hot in here, isn't it? I'm going to ask a series of questions, and I want you to raise your hand if the answer is yes. Alright, let's begin." McMahon fanned himself with his copy of the syllabus. "Actually, I'm sorry. If you could all close your eyes please."

When he closed his eyes, Henry sensed that his leg was awfully close to Carissa's under the table. The energy between their flesh made the hairs on his knees rise.

"No peeking, Mr. Thomson."

"Come on, Frank," Birdie quipped. One or two of the girls giggled.

One time freshman year, Frank bit into a sandwich containing more than an appropriate amount of mayonnaise, and in biting down caused a good deal of the mayo to squirt out onto his hands and all over his lips. The faculty never figured out why his friends always urged Frank to "*come on.*" At lacrosse practice their sophomore spring Coach Francis encouragingly yelled "Come on, Frank!" and practice had to be cut short on account of most of the team uncontrollably laughing their asses off. Or so Henry had heard.

McMahon continued, "Alright. Raise your hand if you often feel stressed at St. Dominic's."

Henry had been in love with Carissa ever since she sang Fleetwood Mac at a school coffeehouse freshman year. Even though it was on a dare, she had sounded heavenly.

"Raise your hand if you often feel stressed, even during breaks and during the summer."

It was enough to send a flush from his heart to down below when Carissa accidentally brushed her leg against Henry's, skin to skin. "*Sorry,*" she half-said as she retracted her smooth leg.

"Raise your hand if you suffer from diagnosed anxiety or an attention deficit disorder."

The only reason Henry had signed up for this stupid AP English Literature class was that he'd offhandedly heard Carissa mention she was going to take it to her friend Tish on their walk to squash practice last year.

"Raise your hand if you suffer from depression, or depressive, uh, what should I call them...depressive *spells*. Be them diagnosed or not."

Carissa accidentally brushed her hand against Henry's shoulder as she went to raise it. In a moment of dimwitted clarity Henry raised his hand after hers, hoping she would hear the ruffle of his sitting up and extending his arm. Henry's heart dropped and skipped and fluttered and nearly flew out of the room before a screech of steel and stone turned his warm tingles into an abrasive shiver. His hand was mere inches away from Carissa's, high above their heads, as he hoped that a perceived bond in mental unhealth might make her want to hook up with him. Their eyes were still shut. A moment passed. Then another.

*It's been a while, hasn't it? Is McMahon writing our names down?*

Pins and needles tingled in the tips of his fingers. More bangs clanged from outside. At least a minute had passed. Henry clenched his hand into a fist and 'accidentally' brushed his elbow against Carissa's forearm. Mission accomplished.

"Oh, shit!" Birdie exclaimed. "Mr. McMahon, are you okay?"

Henry opened his eyes and saw Mr. McMahon on the ground, leaning ungracefully against the wall, and presumably unconscious.

Several kids still had their eyes closed. Two of them (including Carissa) still had their arms raised up to the sky.

/// St. Dominic's Preparatory Academy housed 351 high school students, and another forty students elected to commute. A typical freshman class had between eighty and ninety students. Around fifteen new sophomores arrived each year, as well as a handful of new juniors. About four students dropped out, transferred, or were dismissed each year per grade. ///

# SATURDAY, JUNE 8TH, 2019. 9:42 AM.

———

Sarah wanted to die, or at least fall back asleep. Her hand was already there, all pins and needles dangling off of the bed. The weight of her entire body, it felt, shifted awkwardly onto her shoulder. A flat pillow lay even flatter under her neck.

She texted *I'm soooooo hungover* to the groupchat they'd made for Birdie's party to see if anyone else was awake.

She opened her mouth to yawn, popping her ears with a sound that split her head. Desperately thin strands of saliva connected her teeth.

*Water.*

There was an empty bottle of wine on the ground by the nightstand. She hung off of the bed, extending her arm farther than it should go in an attempt to grab the bottle with her numb fingers. Bright light shone through a gap in the drapes, right at her face. The bottle was too far out of reach.

She was going to have to get up anyway, now that she thought of it. Maybe water wasn't worth it. If she could somehow fall back asleep…

Her alarm went off: 9:45. Bouncing marimba notes pierced her ears. She slapped the nightstand blindly, feeling for the source of the insufferable noise.

"Turn it offfff," a deep voice said next to her, muffled through a pillow.

Sarah jumped out of bed. *Who the fuck?* She grabbed the wine bottle and brandished it in the air, expecting her sleeping partner to reveal himself. Instead, he just began to snore.

Standing there at the foot of the bed, in nothing but her underwear and a t-shirt, Sarah figured she must have hooked up with Frank last night. Carissa would be *so* pissed. Sarah had said she wasn't going to. They hadn't hooked up in months. But maybe Carissa was right, alcohol and hormones throw best laid plans to the wayside. What a fucking bitchy thing to say, though.

There's no way they hooked up last night, come to think about it. Sarah hadn't blacked out. She remembered coming to bed; and she remembered falling asleep. *Alone.*

A rush of panic flushed through her.

She grabbed the white comforter with her free hand and aggressively pulled back it back, revealing a boy lying face down in nothing but his white underwear.

He moaned, and curled into a fetal position. There was still a pillow covering his face, but she knew who it was by the pseudo jew-fro, as he called it, in reference to his curly brown hair.

"Todd?" she exclaimed. "Todd? *What the fuck?*"

"I try...," he said in between heavy breaths. "I fell to sleep on the floor, lasnite." He was slurring his words. "Woke up when sun did 'cause the dog waslicking my face. Came upstairs and passed out. Din' even know, uh, know-*tice,* you were asleeping."

"Todd! Gross!"

"Sorry," he said, face still hidden.

"When did you take your clothes off?"

"Oh, don' flatter yourself, princess. They were off way 'fore I came upstairs."

What a fucking degenerate. Still drunk, even the next day.

Sarah walked to the private attached bathroom, closed the door, and ran the sink. She couldn't fit the wine bottle under the faucet, so she sat down to pee and ran the bath, cold.

Todd said something from the bedroom, but she couldn't make out what it was. Nor did she care to.

After flushing the toilet, Sarah took the wine bottle and placed it under the now icy running tub faucet.

She let it fill up halfway, then chugged. Then she filled it up halfway again and turned off the tub.

In the bedroom she found her jeans under the bed, slipped into them, grabbed her phone charger from the wall, and took one last look at Todd, who was still curled up in a ball with no blankets. Snoring. She took the comforter and threw it over him.

"Thanks," he said. At least that's what she thought he said.

"Don't mention it," Sarah replied. "Actually, don't mention this *at all* either. To anyone. This didn't happen."

"Water?"

"This never happened, Todd. Well nothing actually happened. See? Nothing happened here. Got it?"

"Water."

"Got it?"

"Got it."

Sarah tossed the wine bottle at him after finishing the last of the water. It bounced off of his ass onto her side of the bed.

"You can fill it up in the tub yourself," she said, then went to go find Carissa.

///Todd fell back asleep and finally woke up for the day at 4:00 PM, when Birdie told him he needed to either leave or get his shit together for charcuterie and conversation with the Fayter Family.///

# WEDNESDAY, FEBRUARY 6TH, 2019. 2:55 PM.

———

Carissa wondered if it was *Carissa and Sarah* or *Sarah and Carissa*. It didn't matter, obviously, but either way...

"Is it three yet?" asked Tish.

"Just about," replied Em. "Hey Siri, set an eight-minute timer."

The bus for their squash match against Exeter Academy left at 3:30 PM. Given the time it'd take to walk from her room to the Athletic Center (AC), change into uniforms, and walk to the parking lot, leaving in eight minutes was pushing it.

It was a familiar scene: Carissa sat at her desk cross-legged with her elbows resting on her knees and her chin balanced on her hands, Sarah lay on her bed stomach-down with her feet up, Em and Tish squeezed together on the beanbag in the corner of the room, and Jess sat on the floor, legs crisscrossed, leaning against Carissa's bedpost.

The day had exhausted just about everyone. Cold, soft rain fell on top of the foot of snow they'd received just two days before, making everything bright and gray and thick. The thought of walking to the AC in the pattering rain made Carissa's body sink even further into her desk chair, and her head felt heavy in her hands .

Carissa had befriended Tish and Em through the squash team their freshman year. Tish was the first seed, the best in the school. She'd already verbally committed to play for Bowdoin College in Maine after St. Dom's. Carissa and Em traded fifth and sixth seed depending on their performance the prior game. Both enjoyed playing the sixth seed more.

Jess, initially a close friend of Sarah's, played basketball (though she spent most games warming the bench), while Sarah managed the boys' varsity hockey team.

Carissa yawned, covering her mouth with her hand. Jess yawned afterward, followed by Em and Tish simultaneously yawn-yelling and stretching their bodies by reaching their arms toward the ceiling.

"Carissa, put on some music," Jess suggested as she got up and turned the Bluetooth speaker on. The speaker made a revving sound, to signal it was indeed turned on, then a clicking sound to signal it was paired to Carissa's phone.

"Dreams," by Fleetwood Mac. A family favorite in the Moraine household, which just so happened to translate to something Carissa's friends enjoyed as well.

"I heard something interesting today," Jess said as she sat back down on the floor. "I heard Mark Duplessis ran out of one of his classes, like *sprinted* out."

Em leaned forward. "Caroline was telling me about this at lunch!" she began, "She was in that class, Math with Mrs. K! Caroline says he shit himself, then turned white as a ghost and ran out of class with his hands covering his ass!"

"Caroline Porschia?" Sarah asked.

"No, Caroline Flenser. She says he left ten minutes in and never came back."

"Well you know how Caroline loves to spread rumors."

"I thought that was the other Caroline..."

"Isn't it *shat* himself?" Jess asked, mostly to herself. "Wait. Sarah, didn't Caroline tell everyone she saw you and Frank hooking up?"

"Well, maybe," Sarah said and shrugged. "She definitely told everyone I hooked up with Kevin Yates sophomore fall. Assuming we're talking about the same Caroline." She sat up in her bed as she said this.

"You never hooked up with Kevin?" Jess seemed surprised.

"Well, *yes*, I did. But not until this year. And not that Kevin."

"I heard Mark was in the Health Center today," Carissa said softly. She turned to face the rest of the girls.

"Maybe he's got the shits," Em joked.

Carissa began sheepishly, "Well, I also heard something else... You promise not to tell?"

*Yeah*, they all promised, leaning in to hear.

She said softly: "I heard Mark was drunk, or maybe high? During that class. I heard that's why he's in the Center..."

Em's phone alarm went off.

"Ugh, I *hate* that sound," Sarah complained.

"Anyways, I heard he was there because they're gonna suspend him, or maybe even expel him." The room fell silent as "Dreams" wrapped up. Carissa, Em, and Tish grabbed their coats and Carissa disconnected from the speaker as they started out the door.

"Wait!" Jess beckoned. "Who'd you hear that from, Carissa?"

She turned around. "Grace, of all people."

With that, Carissa and her squash friends were off.

They walked backward rather than straight-on into the gusting sideways rain-turned-sleet. There weren't any real hills on the campus to break up the wind, so often in windy rain umbrellas flew free from their holders. Knowing this (and, in Em's case, having fallen victim to it), the girls walked without umbrellas. A thick fog had settled on the campus since their last class. Not a word was said on the walk over.

Upon finally opening the doors to the blasting warmth of the Athletic Center, Em literally collided into Mark.

"Oh, sorry, Em," he said. "Hi Tish, Carissa…" He was dressed in his JV basketball jersey.

"Do you guys have a home game today?" Tish asked.

"Yeah, against Bell Hill." Mark looked around. "I've gotta get going. Good luck at your squash matches." With that, he walked speedily away.

"Grace is full of shit," Em said as they walked into the locker room to get changed.

"It looks like Mark isn't," Tish joked.

Carissa wanted to say something, anything, but couldn't.

///*Tish won her match 3-0. Em, who was playing the fifth seed, lost 3-2. Carissa, in the sixth seed, complained of a stomach-ache to Coach Terry on the bus and eventually forfeited her match when the time came for her to play.* ///

# THE SNOW DAY.
# 6:02 AM.

———

The fly wouldn't budge.

Mark first noticed it on the mirror above the sink when he
walked into the bathroom. After accidentally splashing a little
bit of piss onto his hands while trying to shake out the final
drops, he resigned to wash his hands. The fly slowly crawled
across the glass, too small to have a noticeable reflection. It
stopped moving once Mark approached the sink, though
it didn't fly away. Nor did it take off when Mark turned on
the faucet.

His one bare foot was cold against the tiled bathroom floor.

The fly was now on his mirrored cheek. Once he finished
washing his hands, he leaned up against the sink and brought
his face closer to the frozen insect. He slowly inched his open
palm closer and held the fly in his reflection. They remained
balanced there, motionless. Mark's eyes blurred in and out

of focus, until suddenly a holler from the hallway disturbed the moment. He'd hardly turned his head before the fly buzzed away.

Upon leaving the bathroom, Mark noticed several of the freshmen on the floor running around excitedly in their underwear and pajamas. When he returned to his room, he was surprised to see Frank and Birdie up and dancing, also in their underwear, backlit by a snowy dawn window.

"Where were you?" Birdie blurted out, nearly out of breath.

Just then Todd burst in the room, matching Birdie and Frank's energy.

Mark asked, "What's going on?"

Birdie, Frank, and Todd formed a can-can line, which Todd invited him to join by placing his arm around Mark's shoulder.

"*Snow-day, it's a, it's a snow-day, snowy-snowy snow day, fuck a school, a snow day,*" Todd sang. "*Phone-phone, called me on my phone-phone, it was Mr. Duncan, said that school was cancelled.*"

Birdie joined in, adding to the verse through the Juul in his mouth, "*I am gonna get so high I'm gonna get so high-high, fuck around and get high, dananana get high.*"

Frank: "*Might just have to join you, just might have to join you, gonna finish my tank, gonna get retarded.*"

"Come on, Mark! Bring us home!" yelled Todd.

And thus sang Mark: "*Bullshit that we even had school, it is MLK day, shouldn'ta even had school.*" They danced and sang and jumped to the sounds of a blissful campus before retiring for even more blissful sleep.

*/// Meanwhile eleven miles away Henry's mother woke her son at 6:15 AM to let him know that school had been cancelled. Henry commuted to and from St. Dom's each day, a thirty-five-minute drive both ways. He missed out on a lot of shit by not living on-campus. One of those things, he figured, was having a close friend. He checked his phone to find two missed texts from Birdie and Frank, both sent at 6:10 AM. ///*

# WEDNESDAY, SEPTEMBER 19TH, 2018. 7:28 PM.

---

Cool air blew in through Birdie's open windows as he picked along on his guitar to "Blackbird" by The Beatles. There was a part in the song where he had to play the fourth fret on the A string and the eighth fret on the B string simultaneously, and his fingers strained to stretch across the fretboard. Blisters bubbled up on the tips of his fingers. He hadn't played the guitar in a long time.

It had been one of those spontaneous bursts of creative energy, whereby Birdie heard something so profound or beautiful in a song (in this instance, the horns in Bon Iver's "For Emma") that he decided he absolutely *must* take out his guitar and try to write, make, play, or do something to harness that intangible, restless creative desire. Today that energy had lasted about twenty minutes or so before Birdie decided he'd be better served learning how to play a more popular song.

At least then he'd have more songs in his arsenal to play whenever his mother (or whoever) asked him to play for them.

The cool gloaming outside coupled with what was sure to be one of the last brilliant summer sunsets of the year no doubt helped bring about this sensation in Birdie—whose heart was still beating faster than usual. He knew that if Mark or Mr. Connolly (who was on dorm duty Wednesdays) or anyone for that matter walked in and disturbed the moment, the wonderful sentimental gush he felt would dissipate—floating out the window toward those final faint glimpses of red on the horizon.

He wondered if he should try to write something down. He pulled up a new note on his phone and typed: *gloaming skies and bug bit thighs // looking for that summertime.*

After reading back what he had just written, Birdie decided that, if he could, he would crumple it up and lob it at the trashcan. Instead, he just locked his phone screen.

*The moment's passed*, Birdie thought. He looked out the window at the pockets of students hurrying back from The Lawn to their dorms for 7:30 check-in. Frank and Chris were walking back toward Langford Dorm (just Lang, in slang). Across three floors in Lang were a mix of freshmen, sophomores, juniors, and seniors. Two faculty members lived there as well: Mr. Connolly in the single apartment, and Mr. Reeves with his wife and two small children in the two-floor apartment on the far east side of the building.

Frank burst into Birdie's room, sunburnt and out of breath, and threw a Spikeball at him. The ball bounced off of the body of

Birdie's guitar and flew up into the air. Frank caught the ball mid-air, then dove toward the large beanbag in the corner of the room.

"What's up, man."

"What's up."

Birdie got up and put his guitar back in its case. He heard Frank ruffling about behind him when a knock came on the door. Knock meant faculty, which tonight meant Mr. Connolly making the 7:30 rounds.

"Come in," Birdie said as he latched his guitar case shut.

Mr. Connolly slowly opened the door and peered inside. This was his first year at St. Dom's. He was maybe in his late twenties, no ring on his finger. English teacher. Dumb glasses that were too big for his face. Brown hair combed slick. Upon finally stepping into the room, clipboard in hand, he looked around and directed a question to Frank in his nasally voice "Why, is everything all right, Mr. Thomson?"

Birdie peered over at Frank, who had rolled his body over on the beanbag. He lay awkwardly on his stomach with his hands by his groin. He turned his head back over his left shoulder toward Birdie and Mr. Connolly.

"Just a little tired is all," Frank said as he slowly rolled onto his back.

Connolly and Birdie shared a glance at one another. Birdie pursed his lips and raised his eyebrows, *I don't know.*

"Very well then," Connolly said as he checked their names off his clipboard. "Get to studying, boys." He took one last look at Frank, who gave him a two-finger salute, and left.

Birdie shot his eyes back at Frank.

"Jesus, man." Frank said. "Give me a little warning before you invite Connolly in next time, huh?"

"He knocked," Birdie shrugged. "Why, what do you have on you?"

Frank reached into his waistband and pulled out several packs of mint Juul pods. He then withdrew a Juul from his pocket and took a deep rip. Eyes closed, he somehow sunk even deeper into the beanbag as he slowly puffed out some O's.

Birdie stood up in disbelief and fear and said, "I thought we said we were better than that." He sat back down on the futon and swatted away some of the vapor lingering loosely in the air, tangential from the O's.

"Yeah, I know we said that." Frank sat up a bit. "We were sophomores then, didn't know better. I tell you, I first tried this at my buddy Chris's house. Middle school Chris, not our Chris. I told you about Chris, right? He's a clown. Anyways, he gives me his Juul and tells me to rip it, that it makes being drunk feel better. So, we're probably like eight or nine deep by this point, so I try it. I cough a shit ton and all that but *it feels good*. My head is buzzing like a bunch of fucking bees, but they're like massaging my head. And my body and fingertips and all that, like, *creak* when I move them. But it's a good creaking. Next morning he gives me an extra Juul he had that he found at a party, and I buy myself a pack of pods that same day. Been hooked ever since."

He'd definitely been rehearsing this little explanation in his mind. A good creaking? Only Birdie could spit out something like that off the cuff.

"Alright, then," Birdie replied. "How do you even get pods? Aren't they banned in Mass?"

"You know how Peter goes to UNH?" Peter was Frank's older brother. Peter got expelled from Groton Academy after getting caught smoking in the dorm a couple years back and finished his high school career in public school.

"So he buys you pods?"

"Yeah, just delivered me some. Cost me $100 for four packs, which is steep, but I'm just glad to have them." He took another rip and looked at Birdie, whose eyes were fixed on the device in Frank's hand. Frank smiled a menacing little smile and waved the Juul in front of his face.

"Nope." Birdie said. "No way. Not for me."

Frank jumped up, still smiling.

"You're fucking stupid," Birdie said as he met Frank's gaze. "*No*, dude. I told you."

Frank crept closer, exhaling cool mint vapor into Birdie's face. Birdie tried with all his might to hold back the smile flexing its way onto his face.

"No, no, no..." And the smile came.

Frank extended the Juul to Birdie.

"Ah, fuck it!" Birdie exclaimed, grabbing the Juul out of his friend's hand. He took his first Juul rip to the sound of Frank cheering.

///The punishment for getting got with a Juul (or any vape) in the dorm or on campus was a two-week suspension for a first offense. Getting caught a second time meant transferring to a public or Catholic school. ///

# TWO

# SUNDAY, JUNE 9TH, 2019. 10:18 PM.

———

*Are you still watching "The Office (U.S.)"?*

Grace stared back at her reflection on the black Netflix screen and wiped a bit of Smartfood popcorn off of her chin. After bidding her family adieu to go to bed (complaints of a headache), she had watched several YouTube video documentaries on notorious serial killers, FaceTimed Carissa, and was now approaching her fifth episode of *The Office*. This was Grace's fourth time watching through the series in its entirety. She was in the middle of season eight—her least favorite season.

*Are you still watching "The Office (U.S.)"?*

She reached for her phone from the windowsill by her bed and opened up Snapchat. Fourteen red squares demanded a response, but they could wait until the morning. After scrolling for something to watch, she landed on the Snapchat story, *Life Hacks.*

Someone used a straightening iron to smooth out a crumpled five-dollar bill. Someone with long bedazzled nails used a quarter to open a can of soda. An ad for American Eagle. Someone tied their dog's leash to their belt loop. An ad for Bitmoji merch. Someone used Wite-Out to paint their nails. An ad for DICK's Sporting Goods. Someone made a spoon out of the foil lid to eat their yogurt. An ad for Xfinity.

*Are you still watching "The Office (U.S.)"?*

She clicked *continue watching* and swiped out of the *Life Hacks* story. She switched to a LADbible story about a teenage girl embracing her body hair and thought about the last time she'd shaved her legs. *Were they really selling Bitmoji merch now?*

Mark called her; she didn't pick up.

*The Office* theme song started to play, and Grace subconsciously hummed along as she threw her phone across the room. In doing so, twisting her body like that, her laptop fell off of its precariously balanced position atop the pink, plush pillow on her thighs. It now lay on its side by her hips. She stayed still, theme song running its course, and considered moving to pick up and straighten out her laptop but ultimately decided it'd be too much effort. It didn't really matter. She could visualize what was happening on screen just from the dialogue. She looked up at the stars on her ceiling remembering that she'd shaved her legs on Tuesday, then closed her eyes.

As she drifted off into sleep, she thought about Friday night at Birdie's house. She thought about Mark in the car, and

Carissa on the roof. She thought about Todd, lying there in the middle of the floor, motionless.

Her thoughts flipped unconsciously into an image of Birdie, balancing a house atop his head. Right as the house was about to tip over, Grace recognized she wasn't in control of her thoughts, and snapped back awake.

*Are you still watching "The Office (U.S.)"?*

*/// Mrs. Martin, her mother, turned the lights off in Grace's bedroom thirty minutes after Grace fell sleep. On her way upstairs to go to bed she noticed Grace's bedroom light was still on and hoped to ask her daughter if her head was feeling any better. The laptop had fallen onto the ground face-down. ///*

# TUESDAY, MARCH 5TH, 2019. 9:09 PM.

___

"Well there's two ways to think about it," Todd said through a mouthful of thick white Juul puff. He'd just been asked the question upon entering the room. He knew his word meant the most; it was upon these hypothetical conversations which Todd thrived. "You could think about it primarily in terms of aesthetics, or you could think about it in terms of practicality. Obviously, you'd outwardly look like a freak if you had two fuckin' appendages growing out of your chest. Like, say goodbye to t-shirts, tank tops…it's bulky winter coats pretty much the whole way through."

"Or a corset," piped Birdie.

"No shot Frank's fitting into a corset," said Chris. "Can I see the Julia Stiles?"

"Not after that little comment, dickhead." Frank threw a pillow at Chris and inched toward Todd, gesturing for the Juul. "Todd, you were saying?"

Todd tossed him the vape and continued: "Right, well, see the other way you'd be able to wear all your clothes and be seen by like ninety percent of the world as completely normal. Practically, though, you'd essentially be impotent."

"So which would you rather be?" asked Chris, who motioned for the Juul.

"You expect one percent of the world to see you naked?" Birdie teased.

It was nice to hold the deciding vote. Todd held onto the tension for a moment longer, perhaps a moment too long, for just then little freshman Miles walked in to return Birdie's HDMI cable.

"Quick, Miles!" Birdie said standing up. "Would you rather have dick-sized nipples or a nipple-sized dick?"

"Oh come on, that's not fair. His body wouldn't change either way!" Todd exclaimed. He still wanted the moment, the vote to be *his* to decide. Frank and Mark were team nipple-sized dick, while Chris and Birdie were in favor of dick-sized nipples. He'd made up his mind: "I vote nipple-sized dick! I'd want a nipple-sized dick!"

Birdie, Frank, and Chris all fell still, staring at Todd. Something was up. Chris began to smile.

"Ladies and gentlemen...," Birdie announced, "we got him!"

"Jesus, bro," Mark's voiced from the top bunk.

Todd's heart sank down to his stomach. "What do you mean? We've got the majority?"

Frank pulled out his wallet and gave Chris five dollars and the Juul.

"What's going on?"

"You fucking dumbass, dude," Frank said. "And who's Julia Stiles?"

Birdie walked over to where Todd was sitting and put his arm around Todd's shoulder. "This is what happens when you skip dinner, dude. Me and Chris bet those guys we could get you to say you want a micro-penis."

*Oh, fucking bullshit.*

"Oh, fucking bullshit!" Todd stood up. "I said I *would* want to have a micro—er, nipple-sized penis. In this hypothetical. *10 Things I Hate About You.*"

"I dunno about hypotheticals, you sounded pretty adamant...," quipped Frank. "What are they, the ten things?"

"Come on, Frank!" Todd pleaded, desperately trying to evoke the old joke at Frank's expense. It was no use. This was going to be a gag for at least the rest of the year. "It's the name of the movie, dipshit."

"Don't you try to deflect this onto Frank. He's done his time. 'Come on, Frank' had its time and place…" Birdie prepared to give the final blow: "But 'go deeper, Todd!' is gonna haunt you like a ghost come football season."

"Wait, what movie?" Frank asked.

Was it worth it to opt out of football his senior year? Todd wasn't getting much playing time as the fifth best wideout on the team, anyway…

Miles was laughing.

It was strange to feel the tears well up. Well, almost well up—Todd fought against that foreign feeling with a considerable amount of might. The knowledge that such a punitive joke, such friendly teasing with the people he trusted most at this school, could elicit such an involuntary response was itself more defeating than the joke. And that fucker Miles, too—"Were you in on this?" Todd asked him with alarming volume, surprising himself. His voice cracked—"were you *iiiin* on this?"

The room fell heavy and silent. Todd was standing up, a good eight inches taller than Miles if you included Todd's hair. His breath was coming audibly out of his nose—could anyone else hear it?

"Todd, cool off, man," said an apprehensive Birdie.

"If Miles was in on this, I might just give you ten bucks," joked Mark from above. He was now sitting with his feet dangling off the bed.

"Isn't that the movie where the Joker sings 'Can't Take My Eyes Off of You'?" Chris asked.

Todd laughed, thankful that someone else had diffused the situation. He mussed up Miles' hair and told him to get out of there, that it was past his bedtime.

Meanwhile, Birdie sang a bastardized parody of Frankie Valli's tune that mocked Todd for having the "cock of a freak."

Frank left with Miles—the freshman to go to bed and Frank to get high and watch *Family Guy*. Chris and Birdie finished the math homework they'd been working on while Mark and Todd sat on their phones. Once his homework was finished, Birdie announced he was going to take a shower by dropping his pants in the middle of the room. Chris left with Birdie, with the intention of calling home from his own room.

Todd wondered when the last time he'd called home was—a week ago? He got up from Mark's desk chair and moved to the futon, where he lay down. This was how these nights would go, all of them just sitting around in Mark and Birdie's room until they decided to retire for the night, or until Mark said it was time for bed. Birdie never called the night off—it was only Mark who ever thought it'd be wise to go to bed.

"Yo," yawned Mark.

Todd figured that was his cue to leave, but it was just too nice laying down. "Yo," he called back.

"Can I ask you something?"

Relieved to not have to get up, Todd said "Shoot."

"What has Birdie told you about MLK Day? The snow day?"

"About your thing?"

A silence.

Todd sat up. "He told me you should've told us, or at least told him, that you'd broken up with Grace."

Mark laughed a little laugh. "That's it?"

He was fishing, and Todd was too tired to bite. "I dunno man, what do you mean 'what has he told me'?"

"Whatever, never mind. I'm going to bed."

Birdie came in just then carrying his towel over his crotch. He tried to shake-dry his brown hair, but it was too short to really send any water droplets flying. "What's up," he said as he opened his pajama drawer.

Todd noticed that people don't *ask* what's up anymore, they just say it.

Mark had turned over in his bed, facing the wall.

"Either of you guys seen my pocket pussy?" Todd asked, to nothing more than a chuckle from Birdie. He sat there silent for another couple of minutes before deciding it was time to hit the hay.

Todd left for the hallway. He lingered for a moment hoping to hear some interaction from the room behind him once he'd shut the door. Several moments of silence later, he went off to bed with a yawn.

*Those two have got to figure something out,* thought Todd as he tucked himself in.

*/// Lying awake in bed, Todd recalled how freshman year Frank had made a joke in music class that Todd's falsetto singing voice was so good only because his balls hadn't dropped yet.///*

# THE SNOW DAY.
# 10:01 AM.

———

Carissa kept a journal. Well, it was sort of like a journal. She'd got it at Target when she was shopping with her mom for dorm supplies before she moved into St. Dominic's for her freshman year. The journal had 365 pages. Every page had a unique question for the day with four sections for responses: a freshman, sophomore, junior, and senior year entry.

The questions ranged from "What color top are you wearing today?" to "Who's the last person you said 'I love you' to?" to "What's your biggest regret of the last year?"

All her freshman year responses were written with a pink pen; sophomore year's responses were recorded in blue. For junior year she had decided on the first day of school (after much deliberation with Sarah) that green would be the emblematic color of the year.

She'd forgotten to fill in yesterday's response, so as Sarah walked in from the shower Carissa asked her, "What class am I enjoying the most right now?"

"This for that journal?"

"Yeah, I missed yesterday's. Last year it was 'Early Modern History' with Mr. T, and freshman year it was 'Drawing I'."

"You mean 'Drawing One'?"

"Yeah, that."

"Unless you're drawing yourself, I guess."

Sarah changed into leggings and a large gray hoodie with "StDMVH" written in bold red letters then put on a pair of fuzzy socks. "Didn't you get, like, a B- in that history class?"

"Yeah, in the end, but I got an A on the first quiz." Carissa bit the end of the green pen.

"Didn't you say Birdie was in your English class?" Sarah asked, but by then Carissa had already written in "AP Literature with Mr. McMahon."

She flipped the page to today's date, and laughed a bit—one of those laughs that's less a laugh and more an indication to whoever may be near you that you want to share whatever it is you're looking at.

Sarah slid into her Birkenstocks and opened the door. "What's today's prompt?"

"'Give yourself a piece of advice.'" Carissa opted to save her response for later.

It was quite the underwhelming snowfall for a snow day. Maybe six inches total, and it had stopped coming down by the time Carissa and Sarah went for brunch. The dining hall was a mammoth wooden building, really beautiful. Lots of long banquet-style tables. There was no formally assigned seating, but everyone knew freshmen sat on the far right side by the cereal, sophomores and juniors sat in the middle, and seniors on the far left side (which was elevated by a single step).

Carissa got herself a bowl of cereal and found Sarah waiting in line for the waffle machine. It took two minutes to cook the waffle, and Sarah was third in line. That'd be at least five minutes.

"Who's here?" Sarah asked.

"Well, there's Dennis and his crew, a whole bunch of sophomores, and then there's Frank, Mark, Chris, and..."

"Birdie too?"

Carissa nodded. "There's a couple open tables, but I don't wanna sit by myself."

"Here, let's go sit with those guys."

"No, it's alright, I'll just wait for you to get your waffle and we can sit together."

Sarah insisted: "I'll just grab a bagel. Come on."

They departed the waffle line and headed toward the boys' table. Frank and Chris sat across from one another at the end of the table. Birdie and Todd were next to them, and Mark was beside Todd.

Sarah shimmied her way in between their table and Dennis' and sat next to Mark. Carissa had to sit, then, across from Mark. Next to Birdie.

"Hello, boys," Sarah said, leaning forward in a near sprawl across the table.

A "'Hi," and "Hello," and "Hey," and "Hellooooo," chimed back from the guys.

Carissa stared at her cereal.

"Ooh, they have Lucky Charms today?" Birdie asked.

Carissa didn't say anything, just kind of made a throat sound: *mmm.*

"Bet," said Birdie, getting up. Frank joined him, leaving Carissa alone on her side of the table.

"I'm going to go make a waffle," Sarah said with a wink.

*Oh, you bitch.*

So there they all sat, Chris, Todd, Mark, and Carissa—forming some strange, stunted "L" around the table. Birdie and Frank were now talking with Coach T and his two little kids by the cereal bar. Sarah had disappeared behind the wall toward the serving area. Chris was scrolling through something on his phone. Carissa's cereal was getting soggy, she realized, so she took a bite.

"How are you on this fine snow day, Carissa?" Todd asked.

"I'm good," she said, though a bit of sugary milk spilled out from her mouth with that over-pronounced "*goood.*" She quickly brushed it off of her chin, yet several tiny, translucent white spots still speckled the table in front of her.

She looked up at Todd, who probably hadn't even noticed. He was on his phone. Mark's pursed smile, however, spoke humiliating volumes.

"Sorry," she said, blushing.

"What?" asked Todd.

*Freshman year: stop apologizing all the time.*

They spoke in fragments about the snow: its lackluster quantity, and how it was bullshit they were even supposed to have school on MLK day, until Birdie and Frank came back with two bowls of Lucky Charms each.

"Where'd Sarah go?" Frank immediately asked.

Todd said, "Omelet."

"No, waffle," Mark corrected.

"Mark's right," Carissa said.

"But she's already got a bagel," said Todd. "Add a waffle, that's a lotta carbs."

"So what?" Frank said, with a bit of contempt in his voice. "She can eat whatever she damn well wants."

"Someone's defensive," Chris teased.

"Dude, I always forget that that happened," said Birdie.

Mark kicked Carissa under the table.

"Ow!"

"Oh, fuck me, I'm so sorry!" Mark said, instantly red in the face. "I meant to kick Birdie."

"Why'd you mean to kick me?"

Frank got up to leave, and Chris followed.

"Oh it's fine. We all kinda forget they even got together too," Carissa said to Mark.

Sarah came back with a waffle. "Henry gives me the creeps," she said, putting her hair into a bun.

"Henry gives me the drugs," Todd said with the same intonation as Sarah's remark. The guys laughed.

"Is your leg okay?" Mark asked.

"Todd, could you get me vodka?" Sarah asked.

"My leg's fine..."

"Depends, will you let me take you out to dinner?"

Laughs from the guys. Mark leaned back in his chair so Todd and Sarah could properly face off.

"Only if you throw in a pack of mango pods."

"Fine, but we split the tab."

"Fine, but you're taking me to Flavio's."

"I hate Italian food," said Todd. "Why don't I take you to a proper steakhouse and give you some meat?"

"Don't be gross."

"The Towne Grille?"

"Tonight?"

"Six o' clock. We'll take the shuttle into town."

Sarah smiled. "Fine. But I'm bringing Carissa with me. I don't know if I could stand an hour alone with you."

*Sophomore year: take control of your life.*

"We'll all go," Birdie said.

"Now there's an idea," Todd said. "Maury'd *love* to hear you're taking his little sister out."

Alex "Maury" Moraine, Carissa's older brother. Carissa thought it was a stupid nickname.

"Mark, invite Grace. We'll call it a triple date," suggested Birdie.

"A triple date," Sarah repeated, eyeing Carissa.

"I don't think that's gonna work," Mark said, leaning back into the conversation.

"Why not?" asked Birdie.

*Birdie wants this to happen.*

"Just not a good time, is all."

"Double date then," Birdie said, standing up. He extended his phone out toward Carissa. "Carissa, my dear, would you be so kind as to give me your phone number so I may properly communicate with you about our evening plans?"

Carissa, who had remained silent for this entire conversation, took Birdie's phone and silently typed in her phone number (triple checking its accuracy, all the while self-conscious about the number of fours in her number).

"Todd and I will pick you ladies up at quarter to six."

And then the boys left, stopping to hassle the freshman lacrosse players on the other end of the dining hall before exiting through the back staircase.

"If I have to hook up with Todd in order for you to get with Birdie, I'm gonna kill you," Sarah said with a smile full of syrupy waffle.

Carissa wanted to cry and scream and smile and jump up and down and run across the entire campus naked and call her parents and strike up a conversation with everyone she saw; her chest fluttered and her feet hovered above the ground and she suddenly had to pee yet she wanted to get a glass of water. She didn't even notice most of her Lucky Charms had become soggy from neglect.

*Junior year: tell your friends you love them.*

*/// Alex "Maury" Moraine: St. Dominic's '18, Harvard '22. Captain of St. Dominic's Men's Varsity Squash (StDMVS), captain of St. Dominic's Men's Varsity Lacrosse (StDMVL), School President, 8x Dean's List, Community Service Chief Student Coordinator, Gunther Prize for Student Leadership recipient '18. Taught Birdie how to play guitar '16. ///*

# FRIDAY, SEPTEMBER 21ST, 2018. 9:14 PM.

———

They hadn't hooked up since the end of summer. The way Mark imagined it in his mind, they'd sneak off from tonight's Crazy Dance to their sophomore year spot behind the dugout. Couples on campus had their own spots. It was a whole thing. Mark and Grace's spot was a stone's throw away from Nick Andino and Maud Fayter's spot by the old soccer net. Mark didn't feel obliged to tell Birdie (or Grace, for that matter) that on several occasions in the spring when a car drove by on the main road right next to the fields at just the right time, headlights a-glare, Mark got a good glimpse of Maud's tits.

Well, now that Nick was school president, he got to hook up in the archives room on the second floor of the library. Each year the school president was given a key to the archives so they could complete their research paper on the school's history (a requirement reserved only for the active president). The paper itself was an inconsequential five-pager that the president had to read to the Board of Trustees during Alumni

Weekend in the spring. It was often written the night before. The archives room had a sinfully comfortable couch which, once one looked past the fact that it hadn't been washed since the seventies, was the perfect place to bring a girl to hook up. It was a coveted honor among the girls at the school to be brought to the archives.

It became a downright competition amongst the guys during Annie Green's turn as the first female school president, class of 2017.

The biggest secret of the archives room—and this came straight from Maury last year, spilling details in the dorm—was the smell. It was a hard smell to place, often accredited to the general must of old texts and relics. Mark had noticed it his freshman year when his history class took a field trip to the room (in fact, Dr. Fielder had commented, "That's the smell of history, folks!"). The source of the smell, according to Maury, was from a prop book at the bottom of a bookshelf on the right-hand wall. The book had a feigned antique exterior, was completely hollow, and could be opened up like a chest.

Inside the book were at least thirty years' worth of condoms, "and you bet your ass they're used" (Maury, 2018).

Now this was top-secret knowledge, passed down from school president to school president. Connor Simpson, school president '16, decided not to tell Annie Green about this tradition. He returned to campus in fall of 2017 to inform Maury of his responsibility as the class of 2018 school president.

All this to say Mark wouldn't be seeing any more of Maud's tits this year, probably.

Mark was thinking about the condom box as Grace said something about the weather. The thought of Maud on that couch…What was Grace saying?

"…do you wanna do?" she finished.

"Whatever you want, hon."

Grace had worn a pair of neon green spandex leggings, an oversized Hawaiian shirt patterned with hula girls and beach balls, a pair of rainbow suspenders, and a cowboy hat to the dance. Being a day student (now with a car!), she could really focus her energies on preparing such elaborate costumes for these themed dances. For Crazy Dance, Mark decided it'd be wild if he wore a pair of sweatpants and a "Life is Good" shirt.

"Ugh, were you even listening to me?"

*Did she really just stamp her foot at me?*

"Of course, you're saying it's cold and rainy. I agree, dugout's not gonna work."

"Glad you're finally with me."

"Hey, I'm sorry, I'm just…," Mark had to say something fast, otherwise it'd be at least another week until he could get some action. "I'm just a little dehydrated, got a headache from all that music and dancing."

"You weren't even dancing! You were just talking with fucking Todd the whole time!"

"That's not true!" *Oh, fuck she's right.* "We danced at the end there! 'All of Me,' John Legend!"

"You got a headache from a slow dance?"

"Let's walk, here," he took her hand. They were outside the dining hall, where the dance was being held. The sound of pulsating music from the other room added a metronome to Mark's patience, which was suddenly wearing thin. Couples occasionally brushed by them on their way to find their secret nook in the school to make out or more.

"No, I don't wanna go somewhere unless we know where we're going!"

Nick and Maud walked by. Maud was dressed in jean shorts and a rainbow tank top with butterfly wings. Mark caught himself staring at her ass as they passed. Luckily, Grace was looking at her phone and not watching his eyes.

"Look, Mark, it's already 9:20. I've gotta be home by 10:30. What's the plan?"

Fucking commuters. The worst.

Mark looked at his girlfriend of nearly two years and was reminded of how much bigger her boobs had become since they got together. She had braces back then, too. "A real snag," per Birdie. Mark was a "goddamn psychic," per Frank.

"Mark," said Todd one afternoon over the summer, "can I borrow the time machine you used to see that Grace Martin would get hot so that I can go back in time and fill out a perfect March Madness bracket?"

"I've got an idea," said Mark now. "In the back of the auditorium there's the green room. Frank told me they don't lock it."

Grace looked Mark in the eyes for a brief moment before turning away. "Fine, let's go."

They walked outside and over to the auditorium in quick silence, light rain falling from above. They passed the night's roamers, Mr. McMahon and Ms. Eliot, who bore their flashlights and ponchos. Each night two faculty members had to roam the campus looking for deviant behavior (namely, kids hooking up) and intervene.

The faculty knew about all the student couples. Hell, Mark was sure they talked about it in their Thursday morning faculty meetings. Gossiping about their students. Placing bets.

They got into the green room all fine, the doors were unlocked just like Frank said. There was an old theater prop couch which wasn't long enough to lay on, but would work just fine anyway. Grace could straddle his lap. It was pitch black inside.

"Which way is the couch?" Grace whispered.

"To the left," Mark whispered back. It was strange that they were whispering despite being alone. They were far out of reach of the roamers who had been walking in the opposite direction, to the parking lot no doubt. Nevertheless Mark's heart was beating fast. Breaking the rules—quite a rush.

Grace stumbled into some large black box on the floor, and Mark caught her as she lost her balance. "Fuck this," she said, taking out her phone.

When she turned on her flashlight, four things happened in rapid succession. First, the two freshmen kids who'd been already hooking up in the green room (and had been absolutely silent this whole time, stunned with fear) appeared topless before Mark and Grace with eyes like startled opossums. Then Grace screamed and dropped her phone. The phone landed face-up, shining the flashlight onto the ground and submerging the room back into its darkness. Finally, Mark went soft.

///Mark had taken two rips out of his dab pen before leaving for the dance, and after he dropped Grace off at her car ("Next weekend, for sure.") Mark went back to the dorm, took four more hits off his dab pen and stayed up till three in the morning with Birdie and Frank playing Fortnite.///

# THE FIRST DAY OF SCHOOL. 8:48 AM.

———

*Ya ill meet u outside the dhall at 8:45*

Henry buttoned and unbuttoned the ass-pocket of his cargo shorts. It was now 8:48; class had been let out thirty-five minutes early on account of Mr. McMahon passing out. Henry had been waiting for over forty minutes outside the dining hall for Todd's arrival. Henry and Todd both had B block free, 8:45-9:25 on Mondays. Todd's money was always small bills crumpled up, sometimes damp.

Todd emerged in the distance, near the pond. He was walking with someone—a girl. Who? Blonde hair, a head shorter than Todd, jean shorts, white top…Sarah Donner? Sarah Donner was Carissa's roommate this year, Henry knew. Sarah peeled off by the main road to head toward Price Hall.

It was another minute or so before Todd made it to the dining hall.

"What's up, man," Todd said. They didn't high-five or dap each other up.

"Good," said Henry. "You?"

"Yeah," Todd put his hands in his pockets. "Alright. Shall we?"

They departed for the car lot, around the dining hall past the science center and behind the Athletic Center.

"Did you see that ambulance earlier?" Todd asked.

"No."

"You don't think there'll be any police around, do you?"

"No."

They walked on, Henry slightly in front of Todd.

"It was McMahon," Henry said.

"What?"

"McMahon, in the ambulance. Passed out during my English class. Probably the heat or something."

"No shit? You saw?"

Henry stopped walking. They were outside the Athletic Center. "No. My eyes were closed."

"What?"

"Just something we were doing. Birdie opened his eyes."

"Huh?"

"Go wait in the boy's locker room," Henry told him. "If anyone asks what you're doing, tell them it's some football thing."

"No one's gonna ask what I'm doing."

"Yeah, but if they do."

"Whatever. Did you say something about Birdie?"

"Don't worry about it. I'll meet you there."

Henry left and made his way to his car, a real piece of shit. Ugly brown Subaru. He reached into his glove compartment and pulled out a black drawstring bag, rummaged through it until he found the orange medicine bottle labeled "Todd," and put the bottle in his backpack then the bag back in the car.

Inside the AC, Henry found Todd lying on his back on one of the benches in between two rows of lockers. A janitor mopped the floors several rows down. The locker room smelled like chlorine and shit.

Henry bought his dank tanks (or, dab pen cartridges—aka carti's) at $900 for fifty. Sold at $35 each, per $900 spent Henry made an $850 profit. He maxed each order at five tanks, as the Adderall prescription bottles could only hold, at most, five tanks. The bottles were used to cover the smell when he sold bud, but he kept the habit even when he switched to the mostly odorless tanks.

The interaction happened in silence: Todd pulling a wad of cash from his pocket and handing it to Henry. Henry unzipped his backpack, pulled out the bottle, and placed it on the bench.

"Yo," Todd said as Henry counted the crumpled bills in his head, *5, 10, 20, 40, 45, 46, 47, 48, 52...*

"Yo," Todd repeated.

"Hold on," Henry had to start over. *5, 10, 20, 40, 45, 46...*

"Any shot you could slide me some Adderall?"

"Hold on," Henry had to start over. *5, 10, 20, 40, 45...*

"I mean you've gotta have some, right?" Todd picked up the bottle and examined it. "Or at least you know someone—"

"I said *hold on*," Henry had to start over. *5, 10, 20...*

"Just wondering."

*5, 10, 20, 40, 45, 46, 47...*

"It's all there. When has it never all been there?"

"Can you just," Henry looked up at Todd. "Give me a minute?"

*5, 10, 20, 40, 45, 46, 47, 52, 62, 72, 77, 87, 137, 142, 152, 172, 173, 174, 175, 176...*

Henry handed Todd the extra soggy dollar.

"Oh, cheers man." Todd picked up the bottle, put it in his backpack, and stood up. "Aight, dog, I'll see you around," and then he was gone.

Henry pocketed the money and went to take a piss.

*5, 10, 20, 40, 45, 46, 47, 52...*

*///The administration used to keep a list of all the students they suspected used drugs. Once the numbers of names on that list exceeded 130 students, or one-third of the student body, the administration discarded that list and started a new one of students they suspected sold drugs or used drugs more than once a week. Somehow, that list wound up longer than the first. The third list the administration put together was of students the school simply wanted gone. Henry's name was not on that final list, nor was Todd's. Curiously, however, Frank's name was near the top.///*

# SUNDAY, JUNE 30TH, 2019. 6:11 PM.

—

Sarah closed her eyes and let the water run over her face. She'd already washed her body and shampooed her hair and, without feeling the immediate need to condition, she moved on to her facial exfoliating scrub. She turned around after rinsing her face and let the water stream onto the back of her head and trickle down her slender body.

She stood with her left leg locked straight and her right leg bent at the knee, right foot resting atop left foot. Her arms were crossed, left over right, on her chest.

*"When I first got to St. Dominic's I was taken aback by…,"* she mouthed, half-whispering aloud.

An Adele song played from her iPhone's speaker, laid upon the back of the toilet and aimed at the shower. The flowing water muffled the song.

"*I'd like to thank my parents,*" she turned to raise the temperature of the water then resumed her position. "*I went to an all-girls middle school. We had to wear those school-girl uniforms. Self-expression wasn't much of an option for us. I remember in seventh grade one girl in my class got detention for painting her nails black.*"

She made a gentle "*shhhh-ch-ch-ch-ch-shhhhh...,*" through her teeth.

"*Detention for dying her hair red...detention for...*"

A memory popped into her mind of a hallway, blue carpets and wooden cubbies, girls congregated in uniform around something, someone.

"*When I arrived at St. Dominic's,*" she continued in barely a whisper, "*I wore incredibly, shall I say, modest clothes—baggy jeans, dresses covering the ankles, things that any father wishes their daughter would wear.*" Pause for laughter. "*Before I arrived at St. Dominic's, I had never gotten below an A- in any class, I'd never been to a football game, I'd never seen a rated R movie, and I'd never kissed a boy.*"

She lightly brushed her left pointer finger up and down her arm.

"*About that last point, for young fourteen-year-old Sarah, it was all I could think about during that summer before freshman year. I was going to go to school with ~gasp~ BOYS!*" Pause for laughter. A bit of water trickled into her ear.

*"I was very eager for my first kiss."*

Rudely, and without consideration for the immense amount of hypothetical reverie transpiring, three loud knocks crashed against the bathroom door.

"What?!"

"Dinner's almost ready! Five minutes!" Her little brother Geoff's wiry voice.

"Okay!"

Sarah wiped her eyes then ran her hands through her hair. *"I was very eager for my first kiss, so eager that I let the first boy that wanted to kiss me, kiss me."*

She turned off the water and quickly reached for her towel, which was draped over the shower curtain. She wrapped the towel around herself and sat down on the shower seat.

*"I let a lot of boys kiss me."* Hold for laughter. Then just say a bit about slut-shaming culture, an anecdote or two, some pieces of advice and a thank-you or two.

Hold for applause.

*///Every Wednesday the school congregated in the chapel to hear a senior give a talk (a "chapel talk," or just a "chapel"). Twenty-two Wednesdays were available for 100 seniors, but only about a quarter of the class actually applied for a chapel. Some chapels were fun, some were sad, the best were both, but*

*almost all of them sucked. A piece of closure for the senior, no doubt; another checkmark in a constructed narrative arc of what a "proper" St. Dominic's experience is like. Sometimes a senior publicly apologized to their ex and sometimes a senior came out as gay, sometimes a senior said the word "'fuck," and sometimes a senior revealed some really heavy personal shit. But most of the time a chapel's impression didn't last longer than the walk from the chapel to third period.///*

# SUNDAY, MARCH 24TH, 2019. 7:52 PM.

———

Henry's thumbs were sweating. He didn't even think that was possible, yet his phone's keyboard was glistening. So far he'd typed and retyped and deleted and almost accidentally sent the message. *7:52*. A reasonable time to ask for homework help.

Would it be weird, though, seeing as he'd had all Spring Break to do this assignment? *Choose one of Hamlet's seven soliloquies and discuss how it relates to the central themes of the play, paying attention to the specific rhetorical devices employed. 500 words.*

He'd already done his writeup. Two weeks ago.

He thought about getting high to help relax, but decided that it'd just make him paranoid.

The words on his screen stared back at him. This was casual enough, right? Doesn't seem desperate? Doesn't seem unnecessary? Doesn't seem, well, what will it seem like? He thought about discarding the message. *7:55.* It was getting late. It was now or never.

*Oh, I'm being such a fucking bitch about this.*

He hit send.

Henry: Hey Carissa, do u know what mcmahon wanted us to do for this assignment?

Carissa had left her phone in her dorm room face up while she went to the bathroom. It was connected to the speaker. Sarah, Jess, and Em were all hanging out putting on face masks in the room and laughing about the fact that Jess looked an awful lot like Spiderus from *Miss Spider's Sunny Patch Friends* with her white exfoliating mask on. The rest of them opted for charcoal masks, which Jess had opposed because, like, "that's just not appropriate," or something.

"Carissa got a text," Em said. She felt the vibration through the desk she was sitting on. "Someone asking about English homework."

Sarah jolted up. "Oh my God, is it Birdie?"

"Unknown number," Em reported. "Could be. Would Carissa have Birdie's number?"

Sarah frowned. "Yeah. Remember MLK day?"

"Oh yeahhhhh," Em and Jess said in unison.

"What's the number? I'll see if I have it saved."

Em read aloud the number. Sarah typed it into her phone. Carissa walked in, face covered in charcoal.

"No, I don't have it."

"You don't have what?" Carissa asked.

"Someone texted you."

"Who?"

"Dunno."

Carissa walked over to her phone and read the message.

Carissa: Who is this?

It'd been five minutes.

Henry blushed.

Henry: Henry

Henry: Dinelli

"It's Henry," Carissa announced to the room.

Sarah laughed. "Dinelli?"

"Yeah."

Carissa: He sent us an email about it two weeks ago

Carissa: You have to pick a soliloquy and write about it

A new fear emerged in the forefront of Henry's mind: *is there any way she'll find out I already submitted it?*

Henry: Thanks

Then the three little dots popped up on Henry's phone, indicating Carissa had more to say. She was going to start a conversation! Henry held his phone far away from him and faced it upward, hiding.

Carissa: How'd u get my number?

He'd planned for this.

Henry: idk it was just in my phone

Henry: probly from freshman yr

Henry: i texted Birdie and Simon abt it but they haven't gotten back to me

Carissa began to unpeel her face mask. The girls went to the bathroom to discard their masks and check out their new skin.

When she got back to her room, Carissa's phone was ringing through the Bluetooth speaker. Was Henry calling her?

No, it was just her Mom. She answered the phone.

Back in his sad little bedroom, Henry watched the minutes pass by. *8:28.* Twelve minutes since his last text. Left on *Read.*

So that was it then, wasn't it? What could he expect, though? Carissa had given him what he'd asked for, and he in turn explained how he had her number. Maybe an "oh okay" would have been appropriate from her. She could've at least done that. Rather than just *Read 8:16.* Maybe it was a glitch, though. Maybe she hadn't actually read it, or she had the conversation open and switched to a different app at the exact moment Henry texted her so that she technically had seen the message but didn't actually see it and was now thinking that it was Henry who was taking a long time to respond. Oh, but that doesn't hold up because he sent three messages over the course of a minute.

Wait, *is she texting Birdie? Asking to corroborate my story?*

Definitely a possibility. Should he text Birdie now, asking what the English homework is? Or is it too late? He could say that he sent the message, but that it didn't deliver. Or he could send Birdie a message right now, and when Birdie told Carissa "hold on, yeah, I just got a text from Henry" then Henry could say "that's weird I sent the text an hour ago."

He thought about Birdie and Carissa having a laugh over weird old Henry.

Carissa: gotcha

Gotcha? Fifteen minutes to think of "Gotcha?"

Carissa: It's so annoying that mcmahon assigned us work over break

Oh, fuck yeah! It *was* annoying. The most annoying thing in the world. It was absolutely mind-boggling that Mr. McMahon assigned homework over break. Henry could talk about how annoying it was for hours. Days. Months. Years. Their wedding vows would be "I will never assign you homework over break like Mr. McMahon did."

Henry: yeah ik! so annoying

Gotta add something, push the conversation forward...

///*They texted for a short while about Mr. McMahon and the class, with a quick "what'd you do over spring break?" thrown into the mix for good measure. Twenty-seven combined texts and an hour and a half later, Carissa announced she was going to bed. Henry had been sitting in his bed clinging onto her every word, crafting perfect responses throughout their conversation. Carissa responded quickly to everything while discussing her plans for the rest of the semester with her friends.*///

# THE SNOW DAY.
# 10:49 AM.

———

Mark grabbed his coats from the rack outside the dining hall and began the long walk back to their dorm with Todd and Birdie.

"Yo, do you guys wanna do shrooms today?" asked Birdie. "If we take 'em within the next hour we should be coming down by the time we pick up the girls."

"You have *mushrooms*?" Todd turned and feigned a gasp, or maybe it was sincere.

"No, but I can get some."

Mark kicked a piece of frozen snow. "I'm down to try them," he said.

*Oh, what the hell?*

///When Birdie picked up his four tanks from Henry before brunch, Henry told him he had some mushrooms in his car if Birdie wanted to buy any. Birdie said he'd get back to him on that, and told him to stick around for another hour or so for Birdie to get some more money.///

# THREE

# WEDNESDAY, OCTOBER 3RD, 2018. 9:45 PM.

————

Frank thought about how damn *good* he looked as he flexed his biceps while washing his hands and furrowing his brow. He had spent two minutes on the toilet just sitting there trying to think of a smart answer to Birdie's question that would impress his friends. The question had been so simple, so open to hilarity and reflection and riffing and all that shit Todd and Birdie were better than him at. He had to think of something.

He left the bathroom, walked down the hall shaking his hands dry, and mouthed *"You guys ready to rock and roll?"* because that's something his dad did whenever he left a restaurant. Sounds of laughter beamed from inside Mark and Birdie's room.

"What'd I miss?" he asked as he opened the door.

"Chris wants to know how many times he's jacked off to the thought of Maud," Mark announced, perched up on the top bunk.

"You took my seat," Frank complained. "But nice."

"That's what I said," Chris said, getting up. "Her butt's nice."

Birdie was leaning against the windowsill, pretending not to notice that the guys were talking about his sister. "So, Frank, did you think of your answer?"

Frank let out a conciliatory chuckle. It was nice to be able to read Birdie like that. "Not yet," he admitted. "How about you guys?"

*Why am I blanking on an answer?*

"I dunno if I'd lock in on this one, but I think it'd be interesting to know how many hours or days I've spent watching commercials or seeing advertisements," Mark said.

"How many fucking jingles have embedded themselves into the fabric of your brain," Birdie added, reanimated by the elegance of his own speech.

Frank pulled out his phone and googled *life stats*. The first link was no good and just told him how many breaths he'd taken after he inputted his birthday.

"Or how many Coca-Cola's I've drunk in my life," from Mark.

"Drank," corrected Birdie. "Or Pepsis."

"Fucking Dr. Peppers," piped in Chris.

The next link was more helpful. Some dumb website, *deep-showerthoughts.com*. "If you could know any statistic about your life, what would it be and why?" headed the page. Exactly the way Birdie had phrased it. Chris and Birdie were saying something. The third reply on the webpage was *how many pounds of pasta I've eaten.* That was pretty fucking stupid.

"How many pounds of pasta I've eaten," Frank said, without knowing why he said it aloud.

"That's pretty fucking stupid," said Chris.

"Yeah, I know."

He put his phone away.

"Frank, you can do better than that," urged Birdie. He always fucking pushed the issue. And there was always an issue.

"I dunno man, like what are the obvious ones? Number of times I've jacked off, number of times people have talked about me behind my back, number of times people have thought about me," Frank said, surprised by how easy these were all coming suddenly. "Miles scrolled on my phone. Time spent looking at my phone—"

"That's the name of a song," interrupted Birdie.

Frank kept on: "Songs listened to. Number of times some-one's said they love me. Number of times I've told someone I love them. Number of words spoken. Number of shits I've taken. Miles ran. Hugs given. Fucking…"

He paused. He realized he was standing up.

"I'm high," said Chris, as though he'd just realized something he'd forgotten.

"We're all pretty blasted," Birdie said. "So which is it, Frank?"

Todd walked in with his backpack on.

Frank sat back down. "Number of times a chick has thought about hooking up with me."

"Zero," chirped Todd.

"Any life stat, Todd. Which would you wanna know?" Birdie posed the question.

Todd sat down on the floor. "Hours wasted doing bullshit schoolwork. Can I get a rip of someone's pen? Mine's dead."

Chris offered his up.

"What about, like, total amount of happiness?" Chris asked as he handed his pen over to Todd.

"What do you mean, 'total amount of happiness'? Can you measure happiness?" Birdie asked.

"I dunno, I'll rephrase it then. Like, total hours spent happy."

"Are you happy right now?" Birdie asked.

Chris shrugged.

Frank ripped his Juul and pondered the question for a moment as well, before quickly landing on *yeah, I am.* He recognized that he couldn't really ponder the matter much further and sunk a little bit deeper into his chair.

"So then how can you find out how many hours you've spent happy if you don't even *know it* when you are happy?"

"I dunno. But isn't the point of this hypothetical that it doesn't have to be stuff I'm aware of? Frank gets to know how many times some chick has thought about his dick, but it's not like he knows it whenever someone thinks about his dick."

"I just always assume *right now*," Frank joked.

"Yeah, okay big guy," Chris directed at Frank before realigning to face Birdie. "Why can't I know how many hours I've spent happy?"

"Well, it's different, Chris," Todd said, having taken his four rips. "If you aren't able to discern yourself when you are or are not happy, then you don't have any metric to base what exactly happiness *is*. A thought about Frank's dick is a thought about Frank's dick, you know?"

"Does that count as two more?" Frank asked, satisfied at being able to think of something clever to add.

"But isn't a happy moment a happy moment?" Chris asked.

"Not necessarily," Birdie said.

"What the fuck are you talking about?" Frank asked, prepared to hear another Birdieloquy.

Sure enough, Birdie cleared his throat. "Aight, hear me out. Happiness is something you can be both conscious of and unconscious of. If you take a moment to think about how awesome it is that you're smackin' lips with a girl, say Grace Martin, you might think to yourself 'I'm happy right now!'"

Mark threw a pillow at Birdie. Todd laughed.

"Alright," Birdie continued, "but then say you're getting dome from some girl, right. Mark, imagine Grace is going down on you. A blowjob is nice, obviously. Getting a blowjob makes you feel happy. But say your mind slips to something else and you end up sitting there balls deep in a hot chick's throat thinking about how she's someone's daughter. You feel guilty all of a sudden. You're thinking about what she was like as a little girl, running around in the summertime. But then, *bang*, she starts doing something different and it feels fucking *goood*. Are you happy?"

"Well,—"

Birdie cut Todd off: "Well, what? Exactly. Well, hold on. Listen. Point is, being happy is a fucked up way to measure happiness."

"Well, Birdie, I don't think any of us are thinking about little girls when we're getting head," Todd said.

Frank laughed, at first because of Todd's quip. Then Frank caught a second wind of laughter when Birdie, for the first time in a long time, didn't have a witty response. He just exhaled and pulled out his phone.

"Everyone at this school is fucking depressed," Frank said eventually. He locked eyes with Birdie, who he knew understood.

"What are you talking about?" Mark asked, sitting up in bed.

"On the first day of class," Frank began.

"When McMahon passed out," Birdie added.

"We were in that class, me and Birdie."

"And McMahon was having us do some dumb ducking exercise about mental health stuff."

"*Raise your hand if you suffer from depression, diagnosed or not,*" Frank said in his best McMahon voice.

"Yeah, right, and we had our eyes closed, and then he just goes down,"

"So we open our eyes, after sitting there in silence for a fucking minute…"

"And *everybody* has their hand raised."

"Except for me and Birdie." Frank concluded.

Chris, Mark, and Todd didn't say anything at first. Todd was staring intently at the floor, crisscross applesauce.

"Wait," Todd said after several silent moments, snapping out of his trance with a visible twitch. "Isn't Henry in that class?"

"Yup. His hand was up too," replied Frank.

"Who else?"

"Carissa," said Birdie. "And a bunch of nobodies."

"Our English class sucks," added Frank.

"What kind of teacher asks all his students to confess their depression *on the first day of class?*" Mark scoffed, throwing a pillow at Todd.

Todd caught the pillow and said, "What kinda student feels comfortable enough to share that information *on the first day of class?*"

"We're living in a fucking simulation," said Birdie. "Have you ever listened to anyone else's conversations? The most absolutely *pedantic* shit you can imagine."

"Nice, that's one of this week's vocab words." Frank still wasn't sure what the word meant since he hadn't studied yet.

"So am I real, or are you real?" Todd probed. "If we are in fact living in a simulation."

"I'm high," Chris said. He was leaning back on the beanbag with his eyes closed, legs apart.

Frank wasn't as high as he wanted to be, but it was nearly 10:30, and he figured it wasn't worth it to take another rip. Well, maybe it was worth it. Probably wasn't, though. Although *Family Guy* was way funnier when he was higher, and he watched that show most nights to go to bed...But, like, did he *want* the show to be funnier if he was just trying to go to bed?

"I know I'm real," Birdie began, "but I can't prove it to you. So I might as well just admit I'm not real, for your sake."

"Okay, I'll do the same," responded Todd. "*I'm not real.*"

Frank ultimately decided to take another four rips of his pen and fell asleep as soon as his head hit the pillow at 11:00.

*///Mark lay awake in bed for four hours, unable to fall asleep on account of a troubled mind.///*

# THE FIRST DAY OF SCHOOL. 9:10 AM.

———

The walk back from the AC to Lang was a long one, and Todd was worried he would run into a Dean on his way. The medicine bottle filled with cartridges of concentrated THC felt heavy in his sweaty palm, tucked inside the righthand pocket of his salmon shorts. Sweat on his sternum clung awkwardly to his dri-fit polo.

Across The Lawn, Nick, clad in his finest summer blazer and white khakis, was chatting with Mr. Duncan, A.K.A. *Dunks*, in front of the chapel. As was tradition, on his first day as school president Nick would give the year's first chapel at 9:30. Dunks, the Head of School, would introduce the students to a great new year before bringing Nick to the podium.

Even from a hundred feet away, the beads of sweat on Dunks' head glistened in the sun.

Todd's new room was on the second floor in Lang. And though he thought it'd be weird to be a floor removed from all of his friends, in the two nights he'd spent on campus he'd come to enjoy his distance. He'd hang out in Mark and Birdie's room until they went to sleep or otherwise kicked everyone out, then retire to his privacy upstairs. The second floor housed Todd and all eight freshman in Lang (already dubbed by Birdie as the "Toddlers").

He swiped his prox card against the detector and entered Lang to a gust of air-conditioned ecstasy. The prox cards were the means by which all the students at St. Dom's entered the buildings on campus. After 7:00 each night, a student's prox card would only work on academic buildings, the AC, and their own dorm. After 10:30, the prox cards only worked on dorms.

The activity of a student's prox was believed to be monitored by Kirk, the school's IT guy. Having no way to prove this theory, Birdie and Frank stole Todd's prox and swiped into Jenson, a girls' dorm, 155 times over the course of two hours.

A student's prox card doubled as their student ID. On each card was a picture of their face, their name, the St. Dominic's logo, and their graduation year. Todd was the only student in St. Dominic's history, it was told, who'd successfully used his prox to purchase alcohol. He convinced the unwitting cashier in his best Scottish accent that he attended St. Dominic's University in Scotland. "Class of 2020" meant he *must* be twenty-one years old.

For some reason, Todd thought about this rumor as he knocked on Mark and Birdie's door. It was true that he once gave a cashier his prox, but it was accidental. He was at a Target, buying only deodorant and a "Happy 50th!" card for his uncle, and had meant to hand the lady his debit card.

Mark opened the door.

"Hiya, Mark," Todd said. "Didn't know you had this block free."

"Didn't know you had this block free either. Birdie's in class."

"I was hoping one of you would be around to check out the—," Todd realized he was still standing in the doorway and entered the room, closing the door behind him with a considerable amount of force. "—check out the recently acquired goods." He pulled the medicine bottle out of his pocket and tossed it to Mark, who had returned to his desk chair.

Mark caught it and examined the label. "How come Henry can't get us Adderall? And why is this bottle so sweaty?"

Todd sat down on the newly setup futon. "Beats me, and have you been outside? It's fucking hot." Outside, the first wave of students were walking toward the chapel. "Who's checking us in?"

"Birdie tells me Stetz is the checker today, but I don't think he'll be doing much checking."

Steven "Stetz" Stetson was a Lang senior proctor and best friend of Nick. Each dorm had a handful of senior proctors whose job it was to keep their dorm-mates accountable to showing up for mandatory events. Stetz would have a clipboard with everyone in Lang's name on it at chapel, and he'd check off everyone he saw. Afterwards, he'd stand outside the chapel, and everyone in Lang would report to him to prove their attendance.

The seniors all sat in the second floor risers at chapel, but friends of the chapel-giver sat in the first few pews. Stetz would doubtlessly be in the front row, trying to make Nick laugh during his speech, unconcerned with scouting out Lang residents.

"I'll text the guys and tell them to tell Stetz we were there after chapel gets out," Mark said with a yawn.

"Good. I didn't wanna sit in that sauna and listen to Nick mumble clichéd this-and-thats and what-have-you's."

Knowing he now had forty-five minutes until his next class, Todd took off his backpack and stretched out on the futon. "How was your summer?" He glanced at Mark. "You and I haven't had much time to chat one-on-one so far."

"Yeah, my summer was good…" Mark stared at his phone.

"That's it? Just 'good'?"

Mark sighed. "I've already got a text from Grace: *Where are you?*"

"Classic. How's that going by the way?"

Mark slowly read his text aloud as he typed it: "*I'm skipping with Todd. Birdie and Frank got us covered.*" He put his phone down on his desk. "Things are good with Grace, things are good." He leaned back in his chair and closed his eyes.

His phone buzzed loudly on his desk. Then it buzzed again. And again. And again. And again.

Mark looked over at Todd. "Things are fine," he said.

Todd nodded. "Cool."

They were both far closer with Birdie than they were with each other. Todd had hooked up with a fair number of girls at St. Dominic's and at summer camps (six total), but he'd never had sex (or, he'd never met the "lucky number seven").

"So have you guys fucked?" Todd blurted out with a smile.

*If we're gonna get to know each other, we might as well get to know each other.*

Mark laughed. "Yessss…," he trailed off. "A month ago."

"And?"

"And we haven't since."

"Had sex?"

"Hooked up. Like, at all."

Todd furrowed his brow and bunched his lips into an inquisitive *hmmm*. "Did you, like, fuck it up?"

"No, no, I mean, like, no. It was fine."

"Did she bleed?"

"It was a first for both of us."

"Did you, you know, finish?"

"We only *did it* for a couple of minutes and then, uh."

"Finished each other off," they said in unison.

"It's probably not that deep, man." Todd said to assure him of his manhood. "Well, actually, I don't know, was it?"

"Was it what?"

"Deep?"

Mark laughed. His phone buzzed again.

Outside the last of the stragglers were making their way into the chapel.

"Alright, I'm gonna jack off," Mark proclaimed.

Todd stood up. "Guess I might too. Do you think Birdie'd mind if I used his bed?"

They laughed. Todd left.

Back in his room, Todd opened up the medicine bottle and attached one of the THC cartridges to his dab pen. He put on some music and internally debated taking a rip.

///*After chapel, Stetz waited in line to hug Nick (there was always a hugging line). To avoid shirking his proctor duties, he gave the Lang clipboard to his younger sister Anna, who was enjoying her first day of classes as a freshman. Young Anna, unsure of what to do exactly, stood outside the chapel as the students grabbed their backpacks and just started yelling out "LANGFORD CHECK IN!" Birdie and Frank walked over, introduced themselves, and checked in. Thirty seconds later, Birdie and Frank walked over and reintroduced themselves as Mark and Todd, and checked in.*///

# FRIDAY, JULY 5TH, 2019. 3:05 PM.

———

The five New Hampshire plates in the driveway told Mark he was in for a real doozy of an afternoon. He wasn't even sure if this was the right house. The address Frank gave him was for Harris *Ave* in Nashua, but Google Maps only recognized a Harris *Drive*. Is this the house Frank would live in? Big in its own right, but the smallest house on the block. Blue, but not blue enough to be making a statement about its blueness. Young Thug playing in the backyard, from the sound of it. Yeah, this was Frank's house.

Mark put his dumpy Volkswagen into park and stashed the key in his pocket. He'd just gotten off the phone with Todd, and interestingly enough they pieced together that they'd collectively seen Birdie's older sister completely naked, if they could merge their memories. Some guys were yelling in the backyard, and he thought he could discern Frank's distinctive bellow from the bunch. He rang the doorbell.

As he anticipated, nobody came to the door. Nevertheless, he rang again.

Nobody came.

He looked inside, wondering what to do. There was an opened thirty-rack of PBR on the kitchen island. Should he just walk around back? Suddenly he wasn't so sure this was even Frank's house. Inside, someone's shadow moved about near the fridge. He rang the doorbell again, accompanied this time by some impassioned knocks.

The figure revealed himself. A tall, skinny kid with wavy black hair, probably Mark's age. He looked at Mark for a moment, yelled something over his left shoulder, and proceeded toward the door.

"Yo, are you Mark?" the guy asked.

He showed Mark inside and tossed him a warm beer. "My name's Rico. We're tossing die out back." Rico opened a sliding door and slipped out, leaving the door open for Mark to follow.

Either Frank's family still had 4th of July interior decorations up or they were extraordinarily patriotic. *Live Free or Die.*

Outside the sliding door was a brown deck overlooking a pristine green lawn. Centered in the backyard was a wooden table with a painted-on American flag. Around the table stood Frank and three of what Mark assumed to be his "wild friends from home," whom Frank often fabled. A solo cup at each corner of the table. Rico sat in one of two red plastic Adirondack chairs positioned near the center of the table.

"Markie Mark!" Frank yelled from a crouched position. "This one's for you! Die!" Frank leaped up and sprung a die from his hand. The tiny cube travelled up and up (Rico yelled "*Moon shot!*") before crashing down near the center of the table, ricocheting toward Rico.

Mark made his way down the stairs and toward the open chair.

"…there's no way, dude, that was *so* line, that's why I didn't even try for it," one of the unknown guys opposite Frank was complaining.

"I'm telling you it was good," said Rico, who had put on a pair of sunglasses. "The line judge's word is final."

"What's up, Mark," Frank said as he dapped him up. He took a deep rip out of a Juul.

Mark sat down next to Rico, who announced the score: "8-7." The guys had crushed about thirty beer cans already and thrown them under the table. PBR. Bud Light. A White Claw?

"Alright, Mark, lemme introduce you to everybody," Frank said. "This here's Ty," he put his arm around the skinny kid standing next to him. "My partner in die. Best friends since we were in daycare."

Ty announced "Die up!" and tossed the white cube, which landed harmlessly on the ground across the table.

"Over there are Benzi on the left and Chris on the right. Benzi is like Todd if Todd weren't so, uh, reTodded…and Chris is a lot like our Chris, but white." Frank laughed. "And you've met Rico."

"Yeah, Rico…" Mark stood up awkwardly. "Sup Ty, Chris, Bonsai—"

"—Benzi," corrected Benzi.

"You and Rico got next game," said Frank. "You're'll like Rico."

Mark wasn't sure if Frank had said *You're like Rico* or *You'll like Rico*, but either way he appreciated how much effort Frank was putting into seamlessly crossing over his prep school world with his townie world.

"Frank's hammered," joked Rico. *Haaaaammerrrrreddd,* just like that.

Mark opened his beer and took a deep sip. "That's not surprising." He figured he'd have about three hours of catching up to do.

"You know how to play Beer Die?" asked Rico, not so much a question of knowledge, but a statement of concerned ability. "I'm not sure how often you can toss at St. D's."

"Yeah, I've played before," Mark lied. "Once. I was hammered though."

Rico cracked open another beer, having already finished the one he just grabbed from inside. Mark figured he'd just try to keep pace now, rather than catch up.

"Ay, Frank. Mark's never played Beer Die before. You told me he was fucking good at it!"

"I told you that so you'd quit bitching about not having a partner!" Frank high-fived Ty. "Oh, but I'm sure he'll be great at it. Wontcha Mark?"

"I *have* played before," Mark tried to clarify. "But I just don't really remember." He felt a tingle in his toes.

"Whatever. We'll still kick your ass, even if my teammate's never tossed before." Rico turned to Mark and said, more softly, "You don't have to lie, you know. Frank learned how to play yesterday."

Mark smiled. "Of course he did."

"Frank, you were in the middle of telling us that story before Mark got here," came from Chris or Bonzi.

"Where was I, Benzi?"

*Benzi. Got it. Stupid name.*

"Something about—"

"Oh yeah," Frank threw his body to the left side of the table and dove to catch a die which had bounced from Ty's corner all the way across the table to Frank's territory. Frank held his hand up high to reveal his triumphant catch, then said to Mark (whom he was sprawled out in front of on the grass), "I was telling them about that time we almost got caught sneaking up to the chapel bell."

Frank stood up and brushed the dirt off of his ass, raised a leg, and farted in Mark's face.

While Frank established mountains of unnecessary exposition, Mark was able to build a buzz. Three beers later, Frank was finally getting to the point of the story.

"Aight so now it's the end of sophomore year, like May 2018."

"We know," chirped Rico. "What's the score?"

"Tied in overtime. Win by two," said Ty, before he threw the die up.

"Let me finish," Frank stammered. He bumped into the table with enough force to wobble the four cups of beer at each corner. Chris's beer spilled over onto several white stars.

"Hey!"

"Hey yourself." Frank picked up his cup of beer and chugged it. "Aight. No interruptions. I'm ready." He put the cup down. "Throw the fucking die." He motioned with his hand *bring it on.* "So at our school there's this chapel…"

Mark had to pee. That fourth beer was trying to break the seal.

"...Right by the pond, you know. Then straight 'head there're all the adacademic, uh, buildings..."

And that damn toe kept tingling, teasing a twitch.

"...Now, what you've gotta understand 'bout boarding school..."

White spots blurred and buzzed at the bottom of Mark's eyes. He closed them, only for his ears to start ringing.

"Lemme teach you how to play before we go on," Rico said, leaning in toward Mark. The sudden speech so close to him caused Mark to jolt, albeit subtly.

"...there's like, these roamers. Faculty. Teachers walk around with flashlights looking for kids hooking up and, like, hooking up..."

Mark's heart jumped a beat, landing on a particularly dramatic thud. His stomach knotted up. It was happening again.

"So on your turn, you throw the die up into the air, higher than like fifteen feet."

"...to the left is the dining hall and then past there is the Athletic Center and the fields. All the dorms are to the right, by the pond..."

Mark opened his eyes. Had he been breathing this loud before? Rico didn't seem to notice.

"The die lands on their half of the table and bounces off, and they've gotta catch it with one hand."

"...all the dorms are to the, on the, uh, right, on the other side of the pond. Lang, the dorm we were in, is brand *spanking* new and right by the waterfront..."

*Fuck me.*

"...beautiful view on one side, shit view on the other..."

"If they successfully catch it one-handed, no point. If they don't, we get a point."

*Ha-ha, fuck me, right?*

"...anyway, me and Markie and some girls decide to sneak to the bells, which is like, a big no-no..."

"If you miss the table, they can kick it up, and if their teammate catches it, they get a point."

It wasn't working. Saying *Fuck me, right?* in your head was something Mark had read once on Reddit. Allegedly quasi-ironic and self-patronizing recognition of a panic attack could help offset its flare-up. But this wasn't a panic attack, this was something deeper. Something primordial. Something he'd brought about in the winter.

"If the die hits the cup and *then* bounces off, that's two."

"...so we get up there, using the master key, and Sarah and I just wanna hook up..."

But it wasn't working, that whole *fuck me* thing. Maybe primordial was the wrong word. This was something *trippy*.

"...but Grace and Mark are with us, so we're just like, *let's sign our names in the bell and get outta here,* you know..."

"And nothing happens if the die lands on the table and stays on the table."

Mark was able to mutter out a hopefully convincing *mmhmm.* He squeezed the armrest on the Adirondack.

"Good, alright here's another rule:"

"...Ty, lemme see back that Juul..."

Mark remembered that night, the way he felt getting back to his dorm. His mind kept replaying it over and over and over and...

"...so we're leaving when *BOOM,* flashlight in my face..."

"If the die rolls back to your side of the table and falls between your two beers, your two goal posts, then that's two points."

The toe twitched. Mark fell back in.

"...*What are you doing? What are you doing? Hey! Answer me!* and all that shit. We all just froze. I'm thinking to myself, *I'm not gonna get head tonight*, and then I'm thinking to myself, *fuck I might actually be in trouble*..."

"If you splash their cup, it's game over."

"...but then what'd you tell him, Mark? Mark? Oh, fuck, Ty, get some water..."

"Oh, shit, man, you good?"

"...fuck, oh, shit, Mark, you remember what you said? Huh? You said, *I'm sorry, Mr. McMahon, we were looking for you!*"

"Frank, what the fuck is going on?"

"...and McMahon was all like, *Is that so*, and you said, *we need an official to time our race around The Lawn. Frank thinks he's the fastest.*"

Mark opened his eyes. Frank was offering him a glass of water.

"...*3, 2, 1, GO!* you said, and then you just started sprinting. So we started sprinting after you."

*Fuck me, it's happening again.*

"...I hadn't run that fast before in my *life*. The adrenaline was ridiculous. You were even faster than me though. Grace was behind, not the quickest. This was back when she was still kinda, you know, *fat*."

"Watch it." Mark grimaced through his teeth. If only Frank could see how hard he was trying to smile.

*Fuck me, it's happening again, and in front of all these people.*

"It's true! She used to be fat. But she got hot that summer. You sniped her freshman year. Shame you only got to be with her while she was hot for a semester."

*Ha! Fuck me, I only got to be with her after she got hot for a semester!*

Mark closed his eyes and took some more stable breaths. He sat there for a while, just breathing and listening. Excerpts of "what's going on?" and "is he okay?" interspersed with bird tweets and overhead jets. He stood up, suddenly, surprising himself. Then he opened his eyes. He wiggled his toe in his flip-flops, regaining control.

"Sorry guys, I get these, like, little flashes sometimes. *Fuck me, right?*"

"Nah, you're cool dude. Frank was telling us just now," said Rico. "You sure you're good?"

"Never been better," Mark said. It wasn't true, but neither was what was happening. He didn't have any drugs in his system; hadn't for months. Complete placebo.

"Alright then, Chris and Benzi just lost, so we're up. You remember what I taught you?"

Mark walked over the table and grabbed a die. He struggled to make a fist. Catching these things was gonna be impossible.

"Of course," he said. He took a step back, his legs a bit wobbly. "Frank, tell them how that story ends."

Frank smiled and opened another beer. "We just ran back to our dorms and laid low. The next day, McMahon asked Mark, *who won?* And Mark, you said—"

"—we won, Mr. McMahon. We won." Mark interrupted. He kicked his flip-flops off and ripped up some grass with his toes. "Die up, I guess," he said before tossing the die as high as he could.

*///Benzi was called Benzi because his first name was Tyler, but there was already Ty and his last name was Benzinelli///*

# THE FIRST FRIDAY OF SUMMER. 6:06 PM.

---

Birdie moseyed on down the stairs whistling a tune, hands in pockets. Steam billowed from the kitchen stove. Carrots, potatoes, steak tips, corn on the cob, and kale salad, from the smell of it. His mother and father were apron-clad, taking pots and pans off heat, salting vegetables and buttering corn. Maud clinked four sets of silverware in her hands, walking from the drawer to the table. On the table were four oceanic placemats, an "Ocean Walk" scented candle Birdie had gifted Mrs. Fayter for Mother's Day, a beach-themed table runner that'd been in the house since the fifties, and several decorative conchs and seashells.

"What's with the fancy table?" Birdie asked, leaning against the kitchen counter.

"Oh your sister's done just such a wonderful job setting the table, hasn't she?" replied Mrs. Fayter.

Mr. Fayter wasn't in high spirits like his wife. "I called you down for dinner five minutes ago, Albert."

"Sorry, I couldn't hear you. I was listening to music."

"We're listening to music too," snapped Maud.

SiriusXM's *Margaritaville* station, if Birdie had to guess. It was unclear how exactly their listening to music negated Birdie's excuse. Maud was just trying to get her brother in trouble.

And that explained why the table was set up so nicely.

"I couldn't hear you, sorry. Food looks delicious, though!"

"Oh, Birdie, next time come down when your father calls you." Mrs. Fayter finished buttering a final cob of corn. "Alright, that should do it. Everybody grab a plate!"

"Yeah next time I can't hear him calling, I'll be sure to answer," Birdie muttered under his breath.

It was hard to deny how delicious the food was. Mrs. Fayter had never taken up cooking before—out of a desire to avoid becoming the stereotypical doting, cooking, cleaning housewife her mother had been. Once she started cooking for herself earlier in spring while Mr. Fayter was away on business, however, she discovered she had an affinity for the culinary arts.

"Would you like a glass of rosé with dinner, honey?" Mrs. Fayter asked Maud once they'd sat down.

Maud took the bottle and poured herself a modest glass. Birdie knew the trick: pour yourself a modest glass, then pour yourself a second glass near the end of dinner (rather than pour a large glass at the beginning). It was a trick he'd used last summer in Italy on a family vacation.

"It's so exciting, now that you've graduated high school I feel like I can finally share a drink with you," Mrs. Fayter exclaimed. They cheers'ed.

"One more year for you, big fella," Mr. Fayter told Birdie in a tone which came off as both a lament and a threat.

Maud would be off to the University of Richmond in the fall. She probably could've matriculated better if it weren't for the fact that her boyfriend Nick was going to UVA. They'd agreed not to apply to any of the same colleges because they didn't want either of their college decisions to be contingent on each other.

The way Birdie saw it, Maud went to Richmond to be close to Nick, and Nick went to UVA to transfer to an Ivy after freshman year. This thought he never brought up to Maud.

"So, Birdie," Mrs. Fayter said eventually after pleasantries around foods quality and the weather were wrought through. "Remind me who's coming tonight?"

He sat up straight in his chair. "Oh, you know the guys. Mark, Frank, Todd, and Chris. Have you met Chris?"

"Is he the black fellow?" Mr. Fayter asked. *Black fellow.*

"Uh, yeah, he's mixed."

Things had changed at St. Dominic's since Mr. Fayter had graduated. They now allowed women and threw around money at scholarships for minorities, as Mr. Fayter might put it after several glasses of cognac. It didn't matter that Chris was the wealthiest friend Birdie had, Mr. Fayter would still assume Chris's success somehow wasn't his own. But was Birdie's success his own? No less than Chris's.

"Oh lovely! I don't think I've met Chris yet." Mrs. Fayter took a bite of salad. "Didn't you say something about girls coming over too?"

"Yep, it's gonna be Sarah and Carissa and Jess and Grace."

"Carissa, would that be Carissa Moraine?" Mrs. Fayter asked.

Birdie knew what she was getting at. He looked at Maud for some backup, but her eyes were glazed over a forkful of carrots.

"Yeah," he began, "yeah, she's the little sister of Maury—er, Alex Moraine's little sister."

Mrs. Fayter dropped her fork on her plate.

"Any news of how he's doing?" Mr. Fayter asked after wiping his mouth with his napkin. "He was a good kid."

"I haven't heard anything since the trial," Birdie said. He realized that he, too, was absent-mindedly staring at a forkful of carrots.

"Let's change the subject," Mrs. Fayter announced. *And that's that.*

Dessert was strawberry shortcake with homemade whipped cream. Birdie realized it'd be best if his father didn't interact with any of his friends.

"Nick says he'll be here in a half hour," Maud said through a mouthful of cream and fruit and cake.

"Are you hip college kids gonna hang out with these high-schoolers tonight?" Mr. Fayter asked in a tone dripping with sarcasm. Something about dessert always sweetened him up.

"We graduated high school *literally* two weeks ago."

"You graduated high school *literally* eleven days ago," Birdie said, mimicking Maud's tone.

Maud kicked him under the table.

"Okay, before your friends come *let's* just set some ground rules." Mrs. Fayter switched to her friendly voice mid-sentence. She hadn't said anything since Maury's name had come up.

"No smoking anything." Mr. Fayter declared. "No cigarettes, no weed cigarettes, no e-cigarettes."

"And no vaping," Mrs. Fayter added delicately. "Or is that the same as an e-cigarette?"

"No smoking vape or e-cigarettes or any of that weed-vape stuff or anything we don't even know about."

"Understood," Birdie said, holding back a smirk. "We wouldn't dream of it. Coke's still on the table, though, right?"

"Birdie!" Mrs. Fayter gasped.

"I was kidding, mom. I wouldn't leave any coke on the table."

"Excellent." Mrs. Fayter said, not getting the joke. He leaned in. "Now, Birdie, will your friends be bringing alcohol?"

Here Birdie was stumped. Before, when it was just Birdie and a couple of buddies over, it had been easy to steal some of his parents' alcohol. The old summer-variety beers in the back of the fridge from last year's 4th of July, the cheap vodka his parents only kept in the house for guests, random bottles of wine from the cellar that weren't worth more than $20 according to Google, etc. Now, with eight friends coming over, stolen booze dregs obviously wouldn't suffice.

This time, Todd and Frank had pledged to use their Pennsylvania fake IDs to purchase enough beer and spiked seltzers for everybody. Regardless, Birdie still anticipated stealing some of his parents' hard liquor once they ran out of the soft stuff.

He didn't know whether to tell the truth and run the risk of his parents confiscating their beer, or lie and risk his parents catching them drunk and assuming they were drunk off stolen liquor.

"Ah, I think so," Birdie managed, "but it's gonna be a low-key evening."

Maud snickered.

"Oh, Maud, at least Birdie's honest with us." Mrs. Fayter snapped. "Will you and Nick be stealing another bottle of wine from the cellar this evening? Or will it be the vodka this time?"

Being the younger sibling, if only by eleven months, made all the difference in Birdie's life.

"Nerd, what time did you say your friends were coming?" Maud asked, disregarding their mother altogether. A bold yet effective strategy.

Birdie stood up, reached into his pocket, and tried to pull out his phone to see when his buddies said they'd be arriving. *No phones at the dinner table* forced each family member to stand up (and oftentimes walk away altogether) whenever they needed to check their messages. In pulling his phone out of his pocket, however, his Juul came out with it, landing underneath the table onto the stone tile with a high-pitched *smack*.

"What was that?" Mr. Fayter asked.

Birdie froze. This was it. He'd made it nine months without getting caught by the school, only to be found out by his parents the first weekend of summer.

"Sounded like it came from outside," Mrs. Fayter said while stacking the dishes. "Birdie! No phones at the table."

Birdie sat back down and began to fish around for his Juul with his feet.

*Got it.* He put his phone back in his pocket and clenched the vape between his toes, slowly bringing it up toward his lap.

The doorbell rang.

"I guess Nick's here early to surprise me," Maud said and giggled, standing up to get the door.

Birdie slid his Juul back into his pocket, underneath his wallet for protection. His heart, though thumping forcefully, had returned to a modest pace.

Behind him, Maud opened the door. "Oh, it's just—"

"Hello, Maud," interrupted a voice which could only have been Todd's signature feigned etiquette. "Birdie! Long time no see. Look what I brought!"

Todd was clad in his finest khaki shorts and pink-striped polo, holding an open bag of Captain Loud's Bang Snaps (those things you throw on the ground with a loud *snap*). Behind Todd, Frank stood wearing only one flip-flop, bent over, massaging the top of his bright red bare foot.

"They work," muttered Frank.

So it began.

///*When the Juul fell out of Birdie's pocket and onto the floor, the pod came loose and detached from the battery. Birdie, distracted by nerves, did not realize this as he scooped the battery up with his toes and placed it in his pocket. It was only shortly after Todd and Frank arrived that Birdie realized there was an errant Juul pod lying beneath the table. On a stealthy rescue mission, Birdie crawled under the table unnoticed by his mother, who was nearby doing dishes and whistling along to Christopher Cross's magical tune "Sailing."*///

# THURSDAY, MARCH 28TH, 2019. 5:15 PM.

———

"They weren't easy to get!"

"I don't care! I wouldn't care if you had to give your left fucking pinky to get them! I wish you hadn't!"

"My pinky toe or my pinky finger?"

"FUCK YOU!"

Mark slammed the door shut and walked briskly down the hallway. Birdie was too much. Always had some comeback, some witty quip, some bullshit he could pull out to mitigate or get out of any uncomfortable situation. It was like that kid refused to just admit that he ever fucked up. Or not even that he fucked up, but that his actions had negative consequences.

But where to go now?

They were about to leave to go to dinner together before they'd started fighting. Should he just go to the dining hall? No, because Frank and Chris were gonna meet them in his and Birdie's room, then all head over together. They were all still gonna head to dinner.

And, nothing against Frank and Chris, he just didn't want to see Birdie. And how would Mark explain it if they were all at the dining hall, but he was sitting alone? Birdie wouldn't want to mosey on over and plop down across from him. No, Birdie was gonna wait for *Mark* to cool down, wait for *Mark* to apologize for overreacting.

For what? Speaking out of turn? Speaking up? God, fucking—

"Damnit," Mark said aloud, to no one, as he exited the dorm. It was spitting rain outside and kind of cold, but he wasn't about to go back to his room to get a jacket. That's not a proper storm-off.

Where the fuck could he go, though? Didn't matter, he supposed. So he just kept walking towards the dining hall, with the intention of walking right past it.

"And it's like, fucking, *god FUCK*," he muttered aloud, again to no one.

There was a wooden bench underneath a massive limby tree by the pond—fuck if he knew what kind of tree. Probably an oak, right? Well it was a big brown tree, anyway.

Even though it was raining, and even though he had no intention of sitting down in the rain, Mark found himself sitting on the bench under the tree. Upon closer inspection, he discovered the tree was actually gray. Most trees, he realized then, were actually shades of gray rather than brown. Using brown crayons in kindergarten was more fun than gray crayons, he guessed.

Oh, but Birdie and Frank and Chris and God knows who else would be walking by any minute now. They'd see him sitting in the cold rain all by himself. How would that make Birdie feel?

Honestly, if Mark couldn't gain Birdie's respect, his pity would do.

So that was the new plan, all formed in as much time as it took Mark to think of the last time he'd seen a gray crayon (never). Wait for those guys to walk by on their way to dinner, have them spot him, tell Frank and Chris how fucked up he's felt since that snow day, and try to elicit some sort of fucking response out of Birdie other than "it wasn't my fault."

Frank would get it; Chris might be confused. Frank had been there, after all. As had Birdie.

Truth be told, it hadn't been Birdie's fault. It was nobody's fault, really. Birdie had tried to blame Grace, but it's not like Grace told Mark he should trip balls after telling him to go fuck himself. Mark at one point blamed Frank, for accidentally playing an ad on the Bluetooth speaker which triggered the whole downwards spiral, but that's a pretty lame scapegoat.

The three of them had left the dorm. T-60 seconds until emotional confrontation.

But how could any of them know what'd been going on since then? It had been nearly two months since the bad trip. Two months of constant re-tripping, often cued by nothing but the fear of something inciting it. Sleep was impossible. Focusing on anything for more than an hour before thoughts of that feeling crept back into his brain was a distant memory.

*Fuck me.*

Thirty seconds.

And it's like, well he should've talked to Birdie as soon as he first re-tripped a couple of days after the snow day. That one was a doozy. Absolutely fucking *terrifying*. One second, Simon O'Malley's passing him a pencil, then the world is twisting inside-out. Mark had almost shit his pants then, or at least he thought he had. So he bolted to the bathroom, abruptly, with no word or indication of where he might be going. Rumors spread, sure, but who cared?

Twenty seconds.

He told the guys that he just *really* had to take a shit.

Maybe Birdie knew that something was up. Mark had been waking up most mornings on the couch, unable to fall asleep in his bed. He'd been zoning out, abruptly leaving rooms to go to the bathroom, going to bed early—those are the kind of things roommates notice.

Maybe Birdie felt absolutely awful in a way his narcissistic mind couldn't reconcile. Thus the deflection, which was juvenile and egotistical even by Birdie's standards.

Ten seconds

Maybe Birdie desperately just wanted to say—

"Are you crazy!?!?"

Birdie rushed over towards Mark, who was shivering sitting crisscrossed on the bench.

"Mark, it's fucking freezing. What are you doing?" Birdie took off his coat and wrapped it around Mark.

Frank and Chris had hung back about twenty feet.

"I'm really fucked up, man," Mark whispered.

"I know, and I'm really sorry this is all happening to you." Birdie helped him to his feet.

"What's going on?" Chris asked.

Mark saw Birdie, like really *saw* him, and saw that he wanted to say, "Mark had a bad trip on mushrooms two months ago and has been living in a constant state of paranoia and misery ever since." Birdie obviously didn't say that. Instead, Birdie said, "Something Mark ate for lunch isn't sitting well, classic fucking St. D's food. He thinks it was the tater tots He didn't tell any of us because, well…"

"Because it doesn't make any goddamn sense," said Mark. He wished it were raining harder so his tears could seamlessly blend in with the raindrops rather than stick out amidst the smaller beads of water on his face.

"Order a pizza?" Frank asked, pointing to Chris. "Order a pizza?" to Birdie. "Order a pizza?" to Mark.

Frank called up the pizza place as they walked back to the dorm. Chris was yelling "With extra dick sauce!" while Birdie tried to tickle Frank's sides. It took Frank the whole ninety second walk back to Lang to order two large pepperoni pies.

Mark still didn't say much until the pizza finally arrived. But hanging out in the dorm definitely beat sitting alone in the cold drizzle.

///Meanwhile, Todd was trying to shove more tater tots into his mouth than any of the other Toddlers in the dining hall.///

# THE SNOW DAY.
# 11:00 AM.

———

Back in the dining hall, Birdie waved at Sarah and Carissa from afar then set off to look for Henry. Birdie found the drug dealing creep sitting alone at a faculty table, eating a bowl of Cheerios with his fingers (and no milk).

"Henrah, Henry, Henrie, Henroh…What's good, my man?" Birdie said as he sat down next to him, putting his arm across his shoulder. "Why are you sitting at a faculty table?"

"You forgot Henruh," said Henry, Cheerio and spittle flying out of his mouth.

"Huh?" Birdie looked around, but the nearest faculty member was Dr. Kerrigan who, with a baby in one arm and twins at her feet, couldn't be bothered to eavesdrop. Most likely.

"Is everything all right with the stuff I gave you this morning?" asked Henry.

"Oh, yeah, no, it's all good. I think. Haven't tested it out yet." Birdie lowered his voice and got in close: "Remember what you were telling me earlier today about a certain magical fungus you might be storing in your glove compartment?"

Henry took a final bite of his cereal and told Birdie to head over to the boys locker room, that he'd meet him there in ten. "It's just a table," he added at the end.

Birdie patted him on the back, got up, said hello to Dr. Kerrigan, mussed up her son Benji's hair (Birdie babysat for Kerrigan sophomore year), waved a final goodbye to Carissa, and left for the Athletic Center.

Ten minutes later, probably to the exact second, Henry popped his head into the nook of lockers where Birdie had sequestered himself. He straddled the bench opposite Birdie and put his knapsack bag in front of him. "So, what were you thinking?"

Birdie's phone's Safari search history included a web forum on proper dosages for first-time trippers. *Take 1.5 grams your first time. Take a full eighth if you wanna transcend. Take 2.5. 1.75. Don't take too much. Don't take too little. Take 1 percent of your weight in pounds in grams. Two percent of your weight in kilograms in grams. Don't worry about it.*

"How much ya got?" was about all Birdie could think to say.

"That's not how this works."

This Henry kid was a fucking enigma. The butt of most jokes freshman year, for obvious reasons. He was five foot two, barely a hundred pounds, glasses, zits, braces, looked like a stereotype of a stereotype of the kid you'd shove in a locker. Then he rolls up to campus on day one of sophomore year desperately peddling drugs. Practically giving them out for free.

Three semesters later, he wasn't giving them out for free anymore. In fact, Birdie knew he was up-charging. But they couldn't just find another dealer in the middle of western Massachusetts. Actually, they probably could. Either way, Henry had too much dirt on just about everyone at the school. Todd said he'd heard Henry yelling at someone in the locker rooms one night, "You can't walk away. I'll get you expelled!"

Where he got his drugs from, no one knew. Obviously.

"Okay, I'll tell you what," he began in his nasally squeak. "I'll sell you two eighths for $50 each."

"Great, I'll take two eighths then. A quarter."

"Nobody calls it a quarter," Henry snickered as he pulled out a scale.

"How would you know?"

*Ah, fuck. Shouldn't've said that.*

"Because I'm a fucking *drug dealer*." Henry pulled some dried mushroom caps out of a baggie and placed them on the scale.

Birdie opened his wallet to find he only had $60 right around the same time Henry finished putting together the bag weighing two eighths, a quarter, seven grams.

"A hundred bucks, then," Henry said and extended his hand.

Birdie leaned over toward Henry. "I'll tell you what—"

"Save it. I don't deal in 'I'll tell you what's.' No IOU's. No favors. No handouts."

"Alright, fine," Birdie stood up. "I'll *let you know* what."

*Did Henry seriously just gulp?*

Standing there, the thoughts all bubbled up through Birdie's body. He wasn't sure where he was going with this, but he knew he'd land gracefully on his feet—with $100 worth of mushrooms in hand.

It was easy to speak knowing what the outcome would be. "Alright, listen here you fucking *freak*. You've done a lot for yourself here. You went from zero to hero, like some fucking twisted building Roman—"

"Bildungsroman," corrected Henry.

"*No fucking interruptions*, kid." Birdie wasn't even sure if he was older than Henry. "Whatever. You used your mind to dig yourself out of the metaphorical lockers we all were throwing you into." *Dig yourself out of a locker?* Of course Henry looked confused. "Never mind the faulty analogy. You think you have leverage over me and my friends and this whole *fucking* school, but you don't. You don't have shit."

Henry put the baggie of mushrooms back into his drawstring.

"Not so fast. You're going to give me those drugs, and I'm going to pay you for them. But I'm not going to pay you $100. That's literal fucking highway robbery, you pepperoni-faced pipsqueak." He paused, surprised how effortlessly his alliterated roast came out. "I only have $60 in my wallet, which I know is a fair price for two eighths, or a *quarter,* of whatever low-grade psychedelic mushrooms you're trying to flip."

"They're actually—"

"Zip it. Now, I'm not in the business of coercion. And I do look to do business with you again, so I'm going to make your end of the deal well worth the drive to school on this magical snow day. You might be able to sleep at night thinking you've got this campus on a fucking string, but I'd bet you lay awake each night with one hand on your dick and another thumbing through Pornhub, am I right?"

Henry said nothing. He wasn't even looking at Birdie, just down at his feet.

"The tissues on your windowsill are used in equal parts to clean up the jizz dripping across your stomach and to wipe away the tears that come when you realize that you might *actually* die a virgin, am I right?"

Oh, fuck. Did Henry really just sniffle?

"Alright, look. That was harsh. I'm sorry. But I'm not wrong. And I can help you. I mean, getting with girls is something my friends and I can do. Well, except for Chris. But that's beside the point. Who do you have a crush on?"

Nothing from Henry.

"Okay, I know who you've got the hots for. I've been watching you."

Henry looked up, red in the face. *Blushing or crying?*

"You could be a little more discreet about it, you know." Birdie hoped Henry wasn't gay. He pulled out his phone and scrolled through his contact list. "Here's her number."

Henry scrambled to pull out his phone. His hands were shaking.

"508-640..." Birdie paused, remembering why he was here. "You get the rest of the digits after you give me the shrooms."

Frantically, Henry weeded through his drawstring to find the bag he'd measured out. Once he found it, he threw it up at Birdie.

Birdie caught the bag and pocketed it in one smooth motion. *Nice.* He put on his jacket and began walking away, all the while announcing the last four digits.

"How'd you know it was her?" Henry asked, his voice echoing across the locker room

Without turning around, Birdie announced, "Because everybody's in love with Carissa Moraine."

It was just convenient he'd gotten her phone number at brunch.


///Back in the dorm, Birdie realized he'd never given Henry the money.///

# FOUR

# SUNDAY, OCTOBER 14TH, 2018. 6:40 PM.

———

Grace caught her mind wandering as the waitress read the day's dinner specials.

"I'm sorry, could you repeat that?"

It'd been twenty minutes already and not so much as a glass of water or bowl of bread had been placed in front of her and Mark. Being one of the only restaurants within a ten-mile radius of campus, Pete's Diner was a St. Dominic's staple.

At Pete's, only two waitresses were on duty at a time. One waitress was always a rotating pretty senior from the town's public high school; the other was affectionately known as the Sea Hag.

Tonight, they got the Sea Hag, which honestly was fine. Grace worried Mark would fall in love with this year's high school charmer as he had with last year's. This was only their second time at Pete's this year, and the first time the high school waitress had been out sick. So Mark hadn't yet been able to check out the talent.

Mark seemed equally as distracted, focusing hard on something over Grace's left shoulder. She turned toward the Sea Hag, just enough to catch a glimpse without overtly gazing.

*Oh, so the new girl's a blonde.*

Grace twirled her brown hair as Mark ordered a bacon egg and cheese on an English muffin with home fries.

"Breakfast for dinner. You kids…And what do you want, *miss*?" The Sea Hag asked, her *sss'sesses* piercing through the air with spittle and haste.

Grace ordered a cheeseburger, "without any of the fancy stuff," i.e. lettuce, tomato, pickle, sauce. Just bun, burger, and a slice of American cheese.

She looked across the table at her lover, who was holding his phone horizontally in his hands. That meant he was either playing a game or watching a video.

*Lover.* What an active word. One who loves. Continues to love. Is in a perpetual state of loving.

She could clear her throat or do something to get his attention, or she could wait to see how long it'd take for him to return his attention to her on his own. She opted for the latter out of curiosity.

Mark was just about impossible to talk to. Well, he could talk about other people, he could talk about St. Dominic's, he could talk about movies and television, he could talk about food. In their two years of dating, Grace had never seen Mark cry, or shout, or otherwise be overwhelmed by emotion. Not that that was a bad thing, of course, or that she was entitled to witnessing such an act. As Mark put it…

How did he put it again? He always changed it. Sometimes it was just that he's not an overly emotional guy. Sometimes it was that he's just always happy, that he has been blessed with outstanding mental health. Sometimes it was just hard for him to relate to Grace when she's dealing with "emotional stuff" because he can't empathize, only sympathize. Sometimes it was because he's Irish. Sometimes he just apologized, with no excuse.

*Will he put his phone down before or after the food arrives?*

To think this was his idea, too. To go out, like old times. Just because they'd been dating for several years didn't mean they couldn't still go on dates, right? He'd complain that he had to pay, though. That's for sure. Even if she offered to pay, or to split it, he'd insist on paying the whole tab. And then, a month later, when she'd be mad at him about one thing or another, he'd bring up how *he's* the one who always has to pay.

But she buys him more expensive gifts! It was great that Mark could write her a poem or orchestrate an elaborate surprise birthday party, but she spent $150 on that drone he wanted, and another $70 on tickets to that Pink Floyd laser show. Not to mention the $50 gift card to The Towne Grille for their two-year anniversary!

Oh, that sure was something. For *his* anniversary present to her, he took her on a date—to The Towne Grille. He used the damn gift card to cover $50 out of the $70 bill.

That was three weeks ago. Grace had thought about making a joke, that Mark had never *actually* given her an anniversary present, but that would start a whole argument about whatever else Mark had stored inside since their last argument.

That was how it went. Grace would bring something up (and it was always *her* who did the bringing-up), then Mark would just unload two or three months' worth of pent-up frustration just to stifle whatever point Grace was trying to make in the first place. And he'd do it with no emotion. Not a frustrated outburst, but a monotone laundry list of cataloged grievances.

Grace was looking down at her lap, biting her nails. She supposed she'd been doing this for a while. She looked up at Mark, who had put his phone away and was now staring at her.

"Hello," he said.

The minutes spent mentally building up her own frustrations with her boyfriend had rendered her speechless to his charmed smile.

"I was wondering," he said, "if you'd say something before our food came."

Fucking prick.

///*The Sea Hag's real name was Martha Bagwell, age sixty-five, beloved grandmother to six grandkids, and regular volunteer at a nearby soup kitchen.*///

# THE FIRST DAY OF SCHOOL. 9:29 AM.

———

Text from Mark, in the groupchat "Lang Gang": *yo can someone check me and Todd into chapel*

Those sons of bitches.

Birdie sat between his sister Maud and the end of the pew. The very first pew. It was a nice gesture and all to be sitting up front in support of Nick, but Birdie didn't appreciate getting stuck in the aisle seat. If he tried to keep his arm inside the pew, it pressed up awkwardly tight against his side. But if he rested his arm on the armrest he looked like a tool (not to mention his hand always fell asleep whenever he did that).

Nick was walking up to the podium, everyone clapping.

Birdie texted back *gotcha, fuck you though* and slid his phone ungracefully into the left pocket of his bunched up shorts. The chapel didn't regulate heat well. There was no central air, no air conditioning. With everyone in such close quarters, early fall and late spring chapels mimicked a sauna. So Birdie dabbed sweat off of his forehead while Nick started talking.

"Hello, St. Dominic's!" he began from the podium. They'd finally installed a microphone over the summer so seniors no longer had to shout their speeches. The hum of students died down instantly, everyone jolted silent by the surprise of an amplified voice.

"I'd like to be the first to welcome everyone to the start of the 2018-2019 school year!"

Applause. *What's the point of those general welcomings?* Birdie mused. *Did everybody need to be verbally welcomed en masse in order to feel welcome? What did that say about the St. Dominic's community?*

"I'm really looking forward to serving as your student body president this year—"

"*WE LOVE YOU, NICKY!*" someone cried out several rows behind Birdie. Probably Stetz.

"I love you too," Nick improvised, visibly caught off guard by the interruption. He cleared his throat and straightened some papers in front of him before proceeding with the obligatory motions of a proper "welcome back!"

After about two or so minutes, he moved on with his chapel. "Who *was* St. Dominic?"

*Ah, yes. Great rhetoric!*

"St. Dominic was Spanish, did you know that?"

*As if his being Spanish mattered.*

"And the man absolutely *hated* comfort. Didn't sleep in a bed, deliberately wore itchy clothes, didn't eat meat, and walked around barefoot. What a guy."

Subdued laughter. Birdie rolled his eyes.

*Did I really just roll my eyes?*

Nick went on to contrast Mr. St. Dominic's asceticism with school-St. Dominic's warmth and hospitality—a lofty and somewhat misguided comparison, but one that garnered enough approving faculty laughter to be considered a success.

"Before St. Dominic's, I went to a local private middle school."

*Here we go.*

It was always the same whenever the senior giving the chapel spoke about their privileged life prior to St. D's. They had straight A's in seventh and eighth grade, they had a lot of friends, and they thought they were passionate about X. Then they come to St. Dominic's, and they got a *B*, and they had to make new friends, and discover a new passion in Y...

"And I lost interest in baseball, but luckily St. Dom's requires us to take four semesters of art electives, so I discovered a new passion: theater!"

It was baffling to Birdie how, for a school that prided itself on its diversity and quirkiness etc., when you really got down to it, everyone was mostly the same. Carbon copies of each other.

"Freshman spring, I had to balance my..."

*Ah, yes. The balance my schoolwork, extracurriculars, and social life bit. Jesus Christ.*

Birdie zoned out. His eyes fixed onto his own shoes, a brand new pair of loafers which were already giving him heel blisters after only an hour and a half.

Maybe it was because St. Dominic's was such an insular community. Eighty-five percent of the students lived on campus. Forty percent of the faculty lived on campus as well. Maybe it's a groupthink, or a hivemind, or something like one of those things they tried to advise Birdie against in those Sophomore Leadership Workshops. Birdie knew his friends were all unique people; Mark was loyal and wise, Frank was loud and loyal, Todd was wise and loud, Chris was...well, Chris was just Chris.

Maybe they weren't as special as they thought they were.

"...and I was able to really come into my own skin on the lacrosse team..."

Maybe they weren't as special as *Birdie* thought they were.

"...only at a place like St. Dominic's can you play lacrosse *and* act in the school play..."

Maybe Birdie wasn't as special as his friends thought he was.

"...and that's when I realized, 'I'm at home here'..."

Maybe Birdie just wasn't as special as he led people to believe.

"...so I'll leave you with some advice: Be yourself no matter what."

Or maybe Birdie just wasn't special at—

*Be yourself? Seriously?*

How can you be yourself? Not everyone was lucky enough to be into such stereotypically polar extracurriculars as lacrosse and drama. How could Birdie *be himself*? Was he not being himself? What was *himself*, and what was so important about it anyway?

"I'd like to thank my parents..."

*No, that's bullshit. Everyone is always being themselves. If you don't have the courage to follow your passions publicly, you're still being yourself. 'Yourself' in that case just happens to be a nervous conformist.*

"I'd like to thank my friends. You know who you are..."

*Be yourself is,* and Birdie hated to use this word figuratively, *literally a call to change who you are. Or at least how you act. As if those are two separate entities, who you are and how you act.*

"Finally, I'd like to thank Maud. I love you, honey…"

Birdie squeezed his sister's thigh, still flustered with his own thoughts. He knew that when he gave his chapel, it'd blow everybody's mind.

*///Birdie would never give a chapel, even though he'd be approved for one. It just so happened that his chapel was scheduled for April 2020. He was offered the chance to give his chapel via Zoom, but he (im)politely declined.///*

# SADTUDADAY, JULE 13ST, 2019; PISSAH LATE.

———

Yeah he was rightly fucked up.

*U know, like, it's been too long since—hold on I gotta text her.*

*Hey, uuu. Iss vebn 2 looong since we see eachoter*

When did the "send" button get so small?

Someone touched his shoulder, pulled him back.

"U black, odd" said…is 'at Birdie?

"Bird, uh, ie!" he belched. "Fuck, dude. I eenta lie down."

*Fuck.* Did Birdie just slap him?

"It's Jim, we went to middle school together. Ur black, odd."

*What the fuh?*

His head got all light like a 'bloon and he ran his hand over his face. Cold skin.

Gotta get outside.

*Fuck.* Corner of the table bumped into his leg.

Someone said "odd's black."

Whoa, he realized he could hear his breaths from his nose. So loud.

Gotta get out—

"Ohmygododd, u aight?"

Just, "yep," and "just otta get..."

Ousside.

*Hooooooooo.*

*Haaaaaaaaa.*

*Hooooooooo.*

And then it all came out, orange and clear and thick. And then more.

"Jee sawed!"

*Bushes.* Gotta get to the—

*Oof.* Fuckin' A, ground hurt. Gotta roll.

Over.

No, stop shaking.

More puke, *great.*

But like *get your finger ow my throat, I alleady puke*

Did he say that though, or just think it?

*Stop* "shaking me."

"You're blacked, Todd. Stay with me."

*I don wanna* "go sleep."

"No sleep,"

*Sleep.*

/ / / … … … … … … … … … … … … … … … . .
*fuck……………..……………………………..///*

# THE FIRST FRIDAY OF SUMMER. 8:00 PM.

———

The sunset over the bay exploded in shades of pink and yellow as Sarah drove over the low bridge separating Birdie's summer community from the mainland. It reminded her of a Strawberry Banana Bash Yoplait Trix Yogurt spiral. Sarah's mom always used to buy her those, and Pop-Tarts, until her Dad offhandedly mentioned Sarah was putting on a bit of weight. She was, like, eleven.

"Hey, do you guys remember those yogurt—"

Grace interrupted her from the backseat to ask if they were close.

"It says we're only two minutes away," Carissa said, co-piloting the drive from the passenger's seat. "Turn left as soon as we're off this bridge."

A Lizzo song played over the Mercedes SUV's speakers. Sarah's phone was connected to the car's Bluetooth system, and they were currently on hour two of her playlist, "Let's Get Turnt."

Grace had complained over an hour ago that Sarah might have jumped the gun in terms of playing hype music. In response, Sarah turned the volume up.

Sarah hated making left turns. She was always worried about the pressure if a car pulled up behind her but there was still oncoming traffic, the threat of getting T-boned if she wasn't careful, the fact that on her first day driving she turned prematurely because she felt pressured by the line of cars behind her—and proceeded to get T-boned. There was no one else on the road, but still she looked around cautiously before turning on Bow Creek Road.

"Birdie's house is number 151," Carissa said, then imitated Siri's voice. "In 1.2 miles, the destination is on your left."

It was good to hear Carissa in high spirits again. Things had taken a turn for the tense after Grace made a joke about Maury earlier. "Remember, girls," she had said. "Let's take care of each other tonight. I don't want to see anyone sloppy. As Carissa's brother can tell you, nothing good comes from sloppy."

"Not even Frank comes from sloppy toppy," Sarah had joked afterwards, but it hadn't done much to brighten Carissa's spirits. Sarah was used to Carissa often being mostly down, down as in sad or something. It was all hard to keep straight, what Carissa actually felt as opposed to what she was *feeling* she felt. At least that's how she'd described it. And Sarah tried her best to keep up. But lately, well since April really, Carissa'd been totally mostly always down, but in a different kind of way. She really had something to be down about, like some *serious shit* to be down about. It was honestly a headache to live with her for the last month and a half. But it was Carissa and Sarah, after all. The duo's name rolled off the tongue almost as smoothly as "Mark and Birdie."

Grace obviously apologized once she realized Carissa hadn't taken her joke well, but it took her a while to realize how distraught Carissa had become. It was easy for Sarah to see Carissa slumped and silent, but Grace didn't have the best angle from the backseat.

So for about twenty minutes they listened to "Let's Get Turnt" in awkward silence before Grace referenced the music's inappropriateness and Sarah turned up the volume.

Sarah couldn't remember exactly when they'd started hanging out with Grace. Carissa got close with Grace before she did, that much she knew. Must've been around Thanksgiving break. She remembered seeing Carissa's Snap story of the two of them playing with Grace's new puppy.

Sarah hadn't received the invite, not that she would've been able to make it anyway. Her family was in North Carolina for Thanksgiving, but still…

And then Grace just started coming over to their room a bunch throughout the winter. Sarah got close with her, as people who spend a good amount of time together do, but Grace only ever asked Carissa if she could come over. Sarah just happened to be there. In the room. *Her* room.

It was nice of Grace to invite her and Carissa over to her house one Saturday night to drink wine and sleep over, but did Grace invite her, or did Carissa?

It was funny, to be driving Grace to Birdie's house to hang out with Birdie and Mark and Chris and Todd and Frank, because Sarah remembered hearing from Jess that Grace had offhandedly called Sarah a slut freshman year after she hooked up with Frank and Todd on back-to-back weekends.

Because Grace was *such* a looker freshman year, anyway.

Like, it wasn't Sarah's fault she didn't have a steady like Grace had Mark.

And yeah, about that, Grace would *not* shut up about seeing Mark that night. She broke up with him five months ago and *still* thought about him. Sarah wasn't sure if Grace still had the hots for him or if she was just nervous to be drinking around him, but either way, it wasn't Sarah's fault, nor her problem.

"79, 85, 87…," Carissa read the street numbers.

Sarah snapped out of her thoughts and realized she didn't remember driving since the turn. It's funny how that works, when you're thinking and driving. It's like you black out, and when you come to, you're like, *was I really just driving?*

The houses, at least the ones that didn't have massive bush fences or long uninviting driveways, were massive. Gorgeous. Wealthy. Carissa's house was nice, and so was Grace's, but these were all proper mansions. Sarah's modest little suburban dwelling didn't hold a candle to any of these estates.

Hell, it was Carissa's Mercedes she was driving. Carissa complained of a headache, so Sarah had offered to drive.

"That's it," Carissa said and pointed. "151."

You couldn't see the house from the street, just a lone mailbox and a driveway twisting toward the coast. About halfway up the driveway, the pavement switched to a coarse gravel.

Birdie's house appeared before Sarah like a revelation. Some great, neo-colonial triumph. Carissa must not have felt the same; she let out a yell of a yawn.

"That's Mark's car," Grace said from the back.

Sarah pulled in behind the Volkswagen and put the car in Park.

"Jess, wake up!" Carissa turned around and yelled.

Sarah had forgotten Jess was even in the car with them.

Inside, Mrs. Fayter greeted the girls to hugs and an offering of snacks, to which Sarah politely declined.

"The boys are in the guest house," Mrs. Fayter said. "It's the little bungalow next door."

That "little bungalow" was bigger than Sarah's house. Music bumped from inside as the girls walked over. Carissa complained of a rock getting caught in her Birkenstock, and Jess yawned twice.

Sarah knocked on the side door, and they were greeted by Chris.

"Hello!" he exclaimed, throwing his arms out for a hug. "Sarah! Jess! Carissa!"

Solo cups were arranged on a foldout table for Beer Pong behind him. Crushed PBRs (gross) had been tossed underneath. A Lizzo song played on what must have been an in-house speaker system, as the music came from multiple directions.

"We were just listening to this song. Where are the rest of the guys?" Sarah asked.

"They're smoking out back, should be back any second. Where's Grace?" Chris asked.

Sarah whipped around. Carissa and Jess had also turned around. Where had Grace gone?

"She might still be in the main house, in the bathroom or something," Jess proposed.

"I don't remember seeing her in the main house," Carissa replied.

Sarah knew where she might be. "I'll go get her," she said.

Chris offered, "You ladies, a White Claw in the meantime?" as Sarah left the guest house.

Sure enough, Grace was exactly where Sarah thought she'd be: still in the car. She tapped on the window, which jolted Grace up. It was dark now.

Grace rolled down the window. "You left the car running," she said.

The dashboard was still lit, the engine indeed still purring. *How did I fuck up turning off the car?*

"I was going to tell you but then you closed the door," Grace said, looking down.

"I don't think that's why you're still in the car," Sarah said. She opened the door and motioned for Grace to scooch over, and then crawled in next to her. "Is this about Mark?"

Grace didn't say anything. Outside, appropriate crickets.

"Listen, we're going to have fun tonight. Although it's gonna suck to see Mark having fun too," Sarah said, ready to give an empowering speech.

Grace turned her head to look at her.

"It's gonna suck," Sarah began in a voice halfway sincere, "but don't let it prevent you from having fun. Maybe you guys will hook up again. Maybe you guys will talk things through. Maybe you guys won't say anything at all to one another. And here's what's worse: maybe he won't even care that you're here. But I'm here, and Carissa's here, and Jess is awake now, and the rest of those guys can be really fun."

Grace exhaled through her nose and smiled, a real-life *lmao*.

"So let's go get drunk—"

"—but not sloppy."

"But not sloppy, and look out for each other, and have fun."

"I can do fun," Grace mumbled.

"I'm not sure you've ever had *this* kind of fun, though." Sarah grabbed Grace's hand and pulled her out of the car. "Let's go!"

"Wait!" Grace stopped.

*After that whole pep talk she still has reservations?*

"The car's still on," Grace said, laughing.

/// When they went back inside, all the guys were there. A Dua Lipa song they'd played earlier in the car was playing over the speakers. Two songs later (that is, two more songs that Sarah already played in the car later), Grace confronted Birdie about the music. He was playing Sarah's "Let's Get Turnt" playlist, because, as he said it, "Now is the time to get turnt."///

# MONDAY, APRIL 15TH, 2019. 7:09 AM.

———

Once Carissa first opened her phone after snoozing her alarm, she didn't cry.

Two missed calls from Mom, 3:11 and 3:13 AM. Text from Dad, 3:35 AM. *Something's happened. Call us when you wake up.*

When Carissa jumped to the conclusion that her grandmother had died, she didn't cry.

Her grandmother had been battling breast cancer for three years. While she'd had her ups and downs, she was on borrowed time and Carissa knew it. She'd said the "last goodbye" at least three times: at the end of the summer, Thanksgiving, and Christmas. So she felt as though she could handle grandma dying in the middle of the night, as fucked up as that seemed. She knew Sarah would want to be a shoulder to cry on, but Carissa seriously didn't anticipate any tears.

St. Dominic's didn't have school today because it was Patriots Day. It was also the day of the Boston Marathon. It was the six-year anniversary of the bombings…had something *serious* happened?

But, she figured, something seriously bad like that wouldn't happen in the middle of the night. Grandma probably just died.

She checked the news (she googled "news"). Nothing cataclysmic had happened overnight. Just coverage of the city's prep for the marathon.

She called her dad, but his phone went straight to voicemail. Should she leave a message? It could probably wait. He had a long night, from the looks of it. He was probably asleep.

She tried her mother. If grandma had died, there's no shot Mom would be sleeping. It was *her* mother, after all, who died. And as much as Carissa and Alex and their Dad knew grandma was on her way out, Mom refused to accept it.

But then why would Mom call twice, presumably after she found out? She'd be in hysterics, most likely. It would've been Dad that called.

Mom didn't answer either, so Carissa sent a text to both of her parents saying "What's up?" and decided to take a shower.

Sarah started to rumble from her bed. "Why are you up so early?" she asked.

"Forgot to change my alarm," Carissa replied, changing into a towel. "I think something might've happened."

"What do you mean?" Sarah rolled over and rubbed sleep from her eyes.

"I don't know. Go back to sleep."

Say Grandma didn't die, Carissa considered in the shower. Was it someone else? If it was Alex, they'd have made a point to wake her up—contact the school, pick her up, etc. Maybe it was one of her older cousins or uncles or aunts, in a car crash or something. She thought about that, the suddenness of it. Explaining it to Sarah, to Grace. To Birdie. "Yeah, Uncle Pete was driving home last night and got hit by an eighteen-wheeler, I've gotta fly to Ohio for the funeral."

When she got back to her room, Sarah was sitting cross-legged on Carissa's chair in her pajamas, holding Carissa's phone. "Riss, something happened."

"How do you know? Did my parents call?"

"No, you forgot to turn off your alarm. You just hit snooze. So after you left, the alarm started going off again. So after a minute I hopped out of bed to turn it off, and then I saw on your lock screen a text from your Dad. I didn't mean to read it, but," and Sarah's voice was speeding up, cracking and squeaking, "and I...just sit down."

Carissa, wrapped in her white towel, sat down on the floor.

"Sarah, what happened? Did my grandma die?"

"No, it's, nobody died. Well, that's not true. It's just, um, Okay, this is gonna sound crazy, I didn't believe it either, but then I googled it, and, well…"

"Googled *what*?" Carissa stood back up, impatient. *What the hell was going on?* "Just tell me!"

"Your brother is in a lot of trouble," Sarah managed. She passed Carissa back her phone.

"Alex? Why? What happened?"

She tried to unlock her phone, but her thumb was still wet from the shower. The scanner couldn't read her fingerprint. She tried to unlock her phone using her passcode, but a few drops of water from her hair smudged across the screen where the "1," "4," and "7" keys were.

*Great day to be born on 07/14/01.*

And why was her password just her birthday? Anyone could guess that. She needed to change it.

"I can't," she muttered, "it's not working."

Pent up with frustration and fuming at herself for her stupid password, Carissa still did not cry.

"Here, use my phone."

Sarah tossed Carissa her phone, already unlocked.

Carissa dried her thumbs on the outside of her towel and opened Safari. She typed in the search bar "Alex Moraine."

She dropped the phone, putting her hands up to her mouth to gasp, but she didn't cry.

She didn't want to leave her dorm room that day. Sarah brought her a bagel and an apple from the dining hall, which Carissa appreciated but couldn't stomach. She'd already thrown up twice. Two hours later, she was still in her towel.

And it's funny how quickly those first two hours passed. After she threw up, she essentially just fell right asleep. Only afterwards, Sarah would tell her that her eyes were open the whole time as she lay naked in her bed, loosely wrapped in a towel, shivering, curled in a fetal position.

Around 10:00 she figured she might need to talk to her parents. She assumed the buzzing from her desk was them.

Sarah asked if this was another episode. Carissa didn't say anything.

Sarah asked if Carissa had been taking the pills. Carissa didn't say anything.

At 11:00 she sat up and drank some of the water Sarah had brought her, and she didn't cry. She put on some clothes (sweatpants and a sweatshirt) and realized she was alone.

She had just supposed Sarah had been lying in bed, on her phone or something.

She looked at her phone and saw the missed calls from her parents. She didn't want to speak to them right now.

There were no texts, no missed calls from her brother. Would he even have access to his phone?

There was, however, a text from Grace. "Hey I know it's last minute but wanna come with my family and I and go watch the marathon?" Sent an hour ago.

So Grace didn't know. Or she did, but was pretending she didn't.

Carissa jolted up with the thought that, for whatever reason, Mr. Duncan would have sent an all-school e-mail explaining what Alex "Maury" Moraine had done. She checked her e-mail, but of course there wasn't anything.

She wanted to go for a walk, as it had stopped raining, but she didn't know who knew. Would the faculty know? Would there have been an emergency midnight meeting? *Last year's school president just did something horrible. What's our response?*

Carissa imagined her teachers, coaches, and guidance counselors reviling in disgust at the very thought…

A thought which, before then, hadn't emerged into Carissa's mind.

She thought of her brother, his face, last night, probably drunk…but she didn't cry.

Sarah came back and gave Carissa a big hug, which Carissa accepted out of respect for the gesture. She didn't need a hug. She didn't even feel the hug. Yet she hugged back, for Sarah.

"I want to go for a walk," Carissa said.

"Okay, let's—"

"Alone, sorry."

"Don't apologize, Riss. It's okay."

If she snuck behind the back of the library, she could follow the old trail through the woods, merge onto the school's cross-country trail and loop back. Two miles, forty minutes. Hopefully no one else would be out there.

Of course, there *was* someone out there. No way the universe would allow something to go right for Carissa Moraine.

"Hi, Carissa," he said.

"Hi, Mark," she answered, and forgot, momentarily, why she was out there in the first place.

*///Later that day, when Carissa finally called her Mom, she didn't cry, despite the sniffles over the phone. When she lay in bed, her mind stirring, she didn't cry. Four days later, at lunch,*

*when she heard a freshman whisper "that's Alex Moraine's sister," she cried and cried and ran back to her room and cried and cried. For what she had felt was true her entire life had become fact: she was in that moment and forever more "Alex Moraine's sister."///*

# THE SNOW DAY.
# 12:00 PM.

---

It had only been forty minutes since Mark and Birdie had eaten the shrooms. There wasn't any clock in the room, but Frank still heard it ticking. Why couldn't Todd be doing this? And why did these guys even need a trip sitter in the first place? What, was Birdie gonna hallucinate that the Megan Fox poster with Sharpie'd-in demonic eyebrows was going to try to kill him? And then what, would Birdie, like, smash a hole in the wall where the poster hung?

Okay, yeah, maybe Frank needed to be here.

"Are you guys feeling anything yet?"

"I mean, I feel a little high," Birdie said, lying on his back on the beanbag chair. "What about you, Mark?"

"I just feel high, yeah."

Birdie laughed. "Hiya!" He karate-chopped the air.

Mark giggled.

When Birdie got high, he didn't shut up; when Mark got high, he rarely spoke. Birdie was silent, as was Mark. Frank didn't know what to make of it. He was just pissed that he'd jumped the gun on starting *The Dark Side of the Moon,* assuming the trip would start almost instantly.

Why would he think that, though? That didn't make any sense. He could be so fucking dumb at times. But he was there, wasn't he? Watching over them, making sure they didn't kill themselves or get caught. They trusted him. He couldn't be that much of a dumbass then, right?

Thirty minutes later Mark and Birdie were on their feet acting retarded.

"You guys are acting retarded," Frank said.

"Hey, man, you shouldn't, like, use that *woooord,*" Mark said, twirling over toward him. "It puts people down. We've gotta lift people up."

That was definitely the drugs talking, but still Frank shrank in his seat. He remembered one time freshman year when he said "that's retarded" in line for an omelette, and two hot senior girls yelled at him and called him an asshole.

You'd think it would have taught him a lesson, but it just made him feel like absolute shit.

Birdie was saying something about something, but Frank couldn't really be bothered to listen.

"I can see through my hands," Mark said. "Frank, watch!"

Frank covered his eyes with his hands. "I'm watching, Mark!"

And this is why Frank didn't want to take any psychedelics, to run the risk of acting this—*goofy.*

Alcohol and weed were enough for him. And nicotine. And caffeine, if you count that. Sugar too. Occasionally an Adderall, if he could get his hands on it. Should beer be counted separately from alcohol? Because Frank didn't drink wine or spiked seltzers or any of that gay, girly shit.

And there he went again, being mildly homophobic. Maybe he just *was* mildly homophobic. He hadn't really thought about it before. He didn't hate gay people, or women, or black people, or any type of people for that matter. But he certainly didn't mind boosting his vocabulary with derogatory terms at the expense of others.

Well, he was genuinely uncomfortable around transgender people. And people with severe mental disabilities. But did that make him an asshole?

"Frank, man, you're just the *best*," Birdie said. "Give me a hug."

Given that Birdie was lying face-down on the floor, the request was probably rhetorical.

Frank was a good guy. He was a good friend. He had a lot of love in his heart, and only teased Chris for being half-black half of the time. But it was in good spirits, right? Hell, Chris laughed half the time!

So what Frank was the dumbest of their little group. He was also the most athletic. And the funniest. Everybody always laughed at his jokes!

That's why he didn't like smoking weed. It made him quiet. He couldn't think of anything to say whenever he smoked. Birdie always out-quipped him when they were high.

"Mark, dude, look at the wood on your desk, man. The knots are *literally* starting to swirl."

Frank perked up. "You guys are hallucinating now? Like, fractals and shit?"

They didn't respond. They were busy looking at their desks.

"Frank, play some Beach House," Birdie requested after another ten minutes. "I'm ready."

Classic Birdie, needs to control everything down to the fucking music. What was wrong with what Frank was already playing? Since when where the god damn *Beatles* not good enough for someone tripping on mushrooms?

He looked up Beach House on Spotify and played the first song, aptly titled something as psychedelically cliched as

"Space Song," and watched Birdie and Mark go catatonic before his eyes.

Birdie sunk into his beanbag chair, practically swallowed by it. Mark lay down on Birdie's bed and covered himself in a soft blanket.

Well, there they go.

Frank opened up *Subway Surfers* and began to play. Birdie had a higher high-score than him by 100,000, and Frank figured now was the time to best him.

Dreamy synths whirled from the speakers. Frank actually didn't mind this song. It beat most of the indie crap Birdie insisted they listen to while high. He looked up for a moment. Mark was twirling his hair, eyes closed. When Frank looked back down at his phone, he had crashed in the game.

*Watch an ad for an extra life?*

Sure, why not.

///*What kind of ad uses a fucking death metal song as the background music?*///

# SATURDAY, OCTOBER 27TH, 2018. 8:50 PM.

———

Grace wiped her forehead free of sweat with her paw. It was awfully hot in the Student Center. Her costume was presumably designed for brisk outdoor trick-or-treating, not close-quarters school dances.

Last year, the weather was so nice that the Student Activities Committee elected to have the Halloween dance outside, in the AC's courtyard. Grace went as a school girl (Mark's suggestion), wearing knee-high stockings, a super short plaid skirt, and a cut-up button-down tied above the belly button. She'd borrowed and slipped on one of Mark's ties from middle school to wear and topped the outfit off with pigtails and thick-rim glasses. Total cost: $40.

The tie had little footballs all over it.

What the Student Activities Committee hadn't planned for, however, was how a warm October day wouldn't translate to a warm October night. After about twenty minutes as Britney Spears' "Hit Me Baby One More Time" classmate, Grace was covered in goosebumps and begging Mark to go inside. Mark, naturally, decided to take her somewhere private. The stairwell by the squash courts. Though she hadn't been in the mood, she was glad to finally be warm.

This year, however, clad in a polyester tiger bodysuit (with a hood!), swamped together with at least 300 other students in the student center, Grace wanted nothing more than to get outside.

She was dancing with her friends Ella and Eva, who though lovely and loyal, were definitely starting to resent Grace for turning beautiful over the summer. Ella was six foot two and thin as a rail, but she had gorgeous hair. Not that the hair was reconciliation for anything beyond easing her drunken laments.

Eva was at least typically built, average height, with nice curves. It'd be another six months or so until she got her braces off.

Oh, but here was Grace embarrassed by the only two people in the world who would go with her as tigers to a Halloween dance. It took forever to find a matching tiger costume that could fit Ella. And Eva did the face paint for all three of them!

She loved her friends, truly. But it was sad to see them so desperately attempting to get some freshman boy's attention. They were juniors now. Juniors weren't supposed to be flirting around the edge of the dance; it was their time to be in the middle!

Grace probably couldn't handle the heat of the middle, come to think of it, and was grateful to be on the outskirts. At least whenever someone opened the door to go outside, she caught a slight gust of cool air.

Eva was dancing right next to some freshman boy...Tim? Tom? She'd met him once before, and before meeting him she'd walked in on him hooking up with some freshman girl. Now, TimTom seemed more interested in the circle of freshman girls in front of him than the junior girl beside him.

Oh, and Ella was closing in behind TimTom too. Good looks.

Grace could go outside, or at least to the bathroom, though she wasn't quite sure how she'd go to the bathroom in that costume. It'd take her friends three songs to notice if she left. Maybe that's because she usually left them to hook up with Mark around now, halfway through the dance.

Wow, was that really all they thought of her?

*Wow, is that really how I am?*

Speaking of Mark, he was over with Todd leaning against the pool table, which had been pushed up against the back wall to clear space for the dance. They were both on their phones. Mark had clearly put a lot of thought into his Tom-Brady-Jersey-and-Sweatpants outfit. He was surely waiting for the "wanna get out of here?" text.

Because it was always Grace's obligation to ask Mark to hook up, even if he (always) wanted to hook up more than she did. It's not that she didn't enjoy kissing and fooling around, but dripping in sweat concealed under a tiger costumes didn't exactly put her in the mood. Neither did being ignored at a school dance.

Like, was one dance seriously too much to ask for?

He'd never text her first, even if his dick was throbbing with anticipation. And why?

*Because I could say "no."*

Grace pulled out her phone from the kangaroo-like pouch of her costume. The palms and fingertips of her paws were made of this sort of mesh that allowed her to use her phone's touchscreen. That's probably why this year's costume cost twice as much as last year's.

It had to be the dehydration and frustration talking, but tonight Grace decided she was going to mess with Mark. She sent him a text: *Ur gonna be wearing ur costume again tomorrow, aren't u?*

Jeez, even her *thumbs* were sweating.

Whatever song was just playing (she hadn't been paying attention) came to an end, and the dancers took a collective sigh before the next song started up. She fanned herself with her paws, flinging droplets of sweat through the mesh of her palm and onto her face.

Ella turned around to check her phone. Her face paint was dripping down her cheeks, now resembling nothing of a tiger's face.

Grace realized that hers couldn't be much better.

*Fuck it.*

She unzipped her costume (which opened in the front) down to right below her breasts and pulled the costume over her shoulders, the sides sagging while resting on her bent elbows. The relief was immense and immediate.

So what, she was exposing her sports bra? Half the girls there weren't wearing much more than their underwear.

One of TimTom's buddies, either Jake or John, turned around and caught Grace fanning herself, half-zipped, JakeJohn gave her a quick up-down.

Where she would normally feel insecure or objectified, Grace felt noticed. JakeJohn was pretty cute—tall, athletic. He was on the soccer team, she thought. A two-year age difference was nothing at a place like St. D's. She could have him if she wanted.

Of course, she wouldn't. Even if she wasn't with Mark, it'd be social suicide to hook up with a freshman boy as a junior girl. Oh, and it'd also be kind of weird.

Mark was still on his phone, yet hadn't responded. If the text had been "let's get out of here," that'd be a whole different—

Someone tapped her on the shoulder. Ms. Flannigan, the new history teacher, was a strapping young twenty-five-year-old alumni, doubtlessly teaching here for a year or two before applying to grad school.

"Hey, Grace, would you mind zipping up your costume?"

*The fucking nerve.*

"It's really hot in here, Ms. Flannigan, I'm just trying to cool off."

"Yes, well, you could go outside to cool off if you must."

*What a fucking bitch.* Half the girls there were twice as revealed as she was now. Maybe it was because she's getting an A in Flannigan's class. God forbid the smart one flaunts her massive boobs in front of the freshman boys.

Still, it'd be nice to get some fresh air. Maybe Mark would notice. He probably wouldn't. At least Ella and Eva…

No, they wouldn't notice either. They were essentially grinding *behind* TimTom.

So Grace snuck out the back door to the crisp October air, alone. She thought about driving home.

"Grace?" someone asked from the grass before her. It was too dark to see.

"Hello?"

"It's Carissa."

Grace walked forward into the darkness before making out a figure lying down.

"Whatcha doing down on the ground out here all by yourself?"

"Care to join me?" Carissa patted the grass next to her.

Grace plopped down next to Carissa, and the two of them lay in silence, staring at what few stars they could see, in the shadow of the Student Center. Muffled dance music became louder and clearer whenever someone opened the door behind them.

It felt nice to be there, with Carissa Moraine of all people. Carissa was the coolest girl in their grade. And the prettiest. At least Grace thought so. She tried to get a glance at what her costume was, but couldn't make it out.

"Sarah left me to go hook up with Frank," Carissa said. "After about five minutes with no one to dance with, I came out here."

Now Grace remembered. Sarah and Carissa had gone as Thing One and Thing Two, respectively, wearing jean shorts and the corresponding t-shirts.

Her phone vibrated on her stomach. She didn't reach for it.

"My legs have been getting devoured by mosquitoes," Carissa continued. "And I'm freezing."

"I'm burning up," Grace said.

"Wanna go back to my room and hang out for a bit? What time do you have to leave?"

"I have time," Grace said. Perhaps too eagerly.

"Sarah has a Juul back in our room."

Though she had never taken a rip of Mark or Birdie or anyone's Juul (and didn't plan on ripping Sarah's), Grace said, "Cool."

"Let's go."

On the walk over to Carissa's dorm, Grace opened her phone to shine a flashlight over the road and avoid stepping in any puddles. Mark's response was just classic: *Why would I wear the jersey tmrw? Pats don't play til Monday night*

To think she'd planned on hooking up with him tonight.

*///As it turned out, Carissa didn't use Sarah's Juul either. She just thought that, because Grace spent so much time with 'Mark and those guys,' Grace would want to rip Juul.///*

# FIVE

# THE FIRST DAY OF SCHOOL. 5:40 PM.

—

It never came as easy for Mark as it did for Birdie. Running a table, that is. Birdie, using only his words and his hands, could completely control the course of a meal. The conversation, the tone, the energy. Whether or not people wanted to get seconds. Mark and the boys had more or less grown weary of Birdie's tricks, but most everybody else were all still suckers.

He knew that underneath all of Birdie's verbose flamboyancies and table-smacking urgencies was a kid who thrived off of control. Without it, Birdie couldn't be bothered to stick around. Someone else was on aux? He'd find other places to hang out. Someone was telling a story he'd already heard? Better check his phone. People were talking about something he wasn't familiar with?

"Yo, what did everybody think of Nicky's chapel?"

See, that's precisely what Mark and Chris and Kevin and Billy were doing: talking about something (NBA 2K) which Birdie was not particularly privy to. So, rather than sit idly by, feigning passive understanding, Birdie needed to interrupt and kickstart a new conversation as if it'd been burning in his mind for too long. His topic of choice: the day's chapel, which he had sat in the front row to hear.

Mark knew all of this because he'd lived with Birdie for two years.

"It was alright," Kevin said. Kevin Moody, good kid. Not by any means someone Mark would turn to in a pinch, but perfect for debating whether or not Nerds Rope is a candy bar.

"Yeah, fine," Frank added. He'd been quietly sitting on the other side of Birdie, on his phone. Probably playing *Subway Surfers*.

"Mark and I skipped," Todd said. Oh, Todd definitely knew how cool he sounded to Kevin and Billy, who would never dream of skipping (much less get away with it).

"You know, it was all kind of humdrum welcome back crap," Billy said. "But it was fine."

Birdie slapped the table, causing a bit of the milk from his bowl of Lucky Charms to spill over. "Fine? That chapel was fucking dogshit. Worst I've seen all year."

"It's the first day of school," Mark said. Birdie obviously knew that and was trying to make a joke. Mark knew he'd have no reply. More importantly, no one would have time to laugh.

Mark wasn't sure why he was trying to undermine Birdie's authority.

"Exactly, and I can't imagine a chapel getting much worse," Birdie responded, hardly missing a beat. "*Be yourself?* What kind of shit is that?"

"I mean he's just saying don't be afraid to be yourself," piped Kevin.

"And who the fuck is that, *Kevin?*" Birdie said, heated. "Who is the real Kevin Moody? Are you being yourself right now?"

Now, it wasn't like Birdie to lose his cool so easily. It'd be best, Mark thought, to let Birdie have a little control here. Wouldn't want to see his roommate embarrass himself.

"Yo, Birdie," Mark said and snapped in his direction. "What the fuck are you talking about?"

"Alright, the way I see it…," Birdie went on for probably two minutes, explaining something that really only Kevin seemed to be paying attention to. "…and that's why '*be yourself*' is a non-statement."

Kevin looked absurdly inquisitive, bordering on mockery. "Say, Mark," he began, "I think Nerds Rope is definitely *not* a candy bar."

"But *why?* We agreed that a Payday *is* a candy bar, so obviously a candy bar doesn't need to have a chocolate!"

Birdie was now on his phone. He would typically devour a conversation this creatively intellectual in nature, but because he'd missed its beginning, he wouldn't feel comfortable jumping in now.

"A Nerds Rope simply lacks the structural integrity found in all candy bars," Kevin continued. "You can bend it into a U without breaking it. Name a candy bar that shares this property."

Mark was flustered; Birdie stood up. "Alright, I yield. Nerds Rope is not a candy bar. But don't act like this is over. We still have no concise all-encompassing definition for what a candy bar is."

"Frank and I are gonna go get some more cereal," Birdie announced.

"I'll come with," Mark said.

Unfortunately, there weren't enough Lucky Charms left for all three of them. Mark opted for Cap'n Crunch instead.

Back at the table, Todd, Billy, and Kevin were fiercely debating rating scales.

"The one to ten is timeless because it's so fundamental," Kevin was saying. "We humans have ten fingers, and they're meant to be used for signaling exactly how-many-fingers hot a girl is!"

"The one to ten system sucks balls, dude," Billy said with grace. "There's no, like, baseline. I could say Em's a six, and you could say she's a four, but if we don't agree on what a five is then we might be saying the same thing."

"You think Em's a six?" Kevin joked.

Todd leaned in. "Boys, let me introduce you to the Todd scale. Very simple. A zero is a girl you don't want to get with, sober or drunk. A one is a girl you'd get with when drunk, but not sober. A two is a girl you'd get with sober and drunk. And a three is a girl you'd only want to get with sober because you'd want to make sure you're on your A-game."

"Sounds like Todd wants to hook up with a bunch of drunk chicks," Birdie said. Everyone laughed, even Todd.

"You know what I meant," Todd said to redeem himself. "Hey, Birdie, Frank, weren't you guys in McMahon's class this morning?"

Birdie told the story of Mr. McMahon's early morning faint.

"...and it was exciting, you know, 'cause we got out of class early."

"Do we know if he's okay?" Billy asked.

"Fuck if I care," Birdie said.

To Mark, and presumably Todd and Frank as well, this disregard for McMahon's well-being was not uncalled for. To Kevin and Billy, however...

"Jesus, Birdie," Kevin said.

"Yeah, that's messed up," Billy added.

Mark threw Birdie a bone: "Birdie and McMahon have some serious bad blood."

Birdie was fishing for a way to tell this story, the *fuck if I care* being the obvious in. He just needed someone to set a bit more context.

"Last year," Birdie began, "McMahon was my English teacher in the spring. And I'm pretty good at English, like I'm a B+/A- student. So I got a B+ on the first paper, then an A- on the next paper. I figure my grade was somewhere close to an A- with participation and vocab quizzes and whatnot. Before our final paper, I go to meet with McMahon. He made us all come in and pitch him our thesis, 'cause it was like an eight pager and he didn't want to have to suffer through directionless slop. Anyway, he asks me if I want to know what my grade was before the paper. And I already have a good idea, like I said, but I say, 'Alright, yeah, what's my grade?'"

Birdie paused to take a sip of his water. Kevin and Billy were clearly hanging on every word. Birdie sure knew how to fucking take a dramatic pause. Even Todd was looking like he hadn't heard the story a hundred times before.

"McMahon tells me," Birdie continued, "'You currently have a C in this class. If you get an A on this paper, however, you can bump that up to a B-.'"

"What the fuck?"

"Why a C?"

Birdie always allotted proper time for rhetorical questioning. "So I ask McMahon, you know, *what the fuck? Why a C?* And you know what he says to me? He says, 'Albert, you have several outstanding assignments.' So I look at him, right, I look him dead in the eye, and I say, 'I know my work is outstanding. What's your point?'"

"But he meant—"

"—not that kind of outstanding."

"Turns out, because I switched into the class at the semester break, there were these weekly online reflection pieces we were supposed to be doing. I hadn't done a single one. So I ended up with a B- in that class." Birdie finished his orange juice. "Wait, did you say I'm kind of not that outstanding?"

///McMahon had indeed sent Birdie several e-mail reminders about the reflection pieces, even offering a grace period whereby Birdie could get full credit so long as he completed them all by the end of the year. Of course, Birdie didn't check his e-mail, and when he did, didn't open e-mails from Mr. McMahon. If whatever McMahon had to say were truly important, he'd say it in class the next day.///

# SUNDAY, JULY 28TH, 2019. 6:49 PM.

———

Frank knew he had to hit up the fellas. This was big news.

**Groupchat: STD Enthusiasts**

Frank: yo did anyone else see henrys story?

Birdo (Yoshi's Pink Piece): Dude I was literally just about to ask

Mr. Pussywhipped: Snap or Insta?

Birdo (Yoshi's Pink Piece): Snap

Frank: lmao mark ur still mr pussywhipped on my phone

Mr. Pussywhipped: Yea u should def change that

Birdo (Yoshi's Pink Piece): Am I still yoshi's pink piece?

Toodles laughed at "Am I still yoshi's pink piece?"

Toodles: what does that even mean?

Frank: like birdo, from mario. yoshi's gf

Frank: fuck it i'll change it its too long anyway it cuts off …
on my phone lmao

Marky Mark: Holy shit, when did henry get expelled?

Chris: Frank what's my name in your phone?

Toodles: where are we gonna get our drugs now lol

Frank: just Chris

Chris: Good

Toodles: am i still toodles

Frank: of course

Alberto: Has anyone heard from henry since graduation?

Marky Mark: Fuck now that I'm thinking about it I saw him
talking with welsh at graduation

Alberto: Did he look chummy or like 'oh shit I just
got expelled'

Marky Mark: Does Henry ever look chummy?

Toodles laughed at "Does Henry ever look chummy?"

Frank: im talking with carissa abt it too, shes talking with the girls

Alberto: Lets just switch groupchats then

Alberto: To the one we had for my party

Toodles: but i don't wanna talk with girls

Toodles: they have cooties

Frank: shut up toodles

Chris laughed at "Does Henry ever look chummy?"

Chris laughed at "they have cooties"

Chris laughed at "shut up toodles"

Frank had to scroll down in his text log quite a ways before finding the groupchat "Birdie's party," last message sent 6/8/19.

**Groupchat: Birdie's party**

Frank: yo yo yo RIP henry

Carissa: So sad!

Alberto: RIP a true legend

Jess: omg when did this happen???

Marky Mark: Maybe at graduation

Grace: Yeah I saw henry at graduation walking with Mr. Welsh

Toodles laughed at "I'm soooooo hungover"

Alberto laughed at "Todd laughed at "I'm soooooo hungover"

Grace: He definitely had that 'i just got expelled' look on his face

Marky Mark: Remember when rodrigo got expelled sophomore year?

Toodles: dude looked like he'd shat himself

Jess: gross

Frank: henry lived nearby right?

Grace: Yeah he was a day student

Alberto: Maybe he could still supply us with our needed goods

Toodles: u really think he's about to start selling again?

Alberto: Maybe he got expelled for something else

My Darling Sarah: wtf else would henry dinelli get expelled for

Toodles: maybe they found the cameras he put in the girls showers

Grace: WHAT

Alberto laughed at "maybe they found the cameras he put in the girls showers"

Alberto: Todd ur really gonna let henry take the fall for that?

Carissa: What are you guys talking about???

Frank: todd you spilled the beans

*You removed Toodles from the conversation.*

Marky Mark: Lol

Chris laughed at "Alberto laughed at "Todd laughed at "I'm soooooo hungover"

**Groupchat: STD Enthusiasts**

Toodles: dude

Alberto: Lol u don't think they actually think there are cameras in the showers right?

Marky Mark: Shit grace might not have gotten the joke

Frank: Lovers quarrel?

Marky Mark: Fuck off

Toodles: frank add me back

**Groupchat: Birdie's party**

*You added Toodles to the conversation.*

Frank: aight todd u back

Jess: I hope henry is okay

Alberto: Henry was never okay

Carissa laughed at "Henry was never okay"

My Darling Sarah emphasized "Henry was never okay"

Marky Mark: We've been broken up for like six months dude

Frank laughed at "We've been broken up for like six months dude"

**Groupchat: STD Enthusiasts**

Marky Mark: Holy shit fuck me I sent that in the wrong groupchat

Frank: lmao retard

Alberto emphasized "lmao retard"

**Groupchat: Birdie's party**

Frank: mark it's only been like 3 months since we bought from henry

Marky Mark liked "mark it's only been like 3 months since we bought from henry"

**Groupchat: STD Enthusiasts**

Marky Mark: Thanks Frank

**Groupchat: Birdie's party**

Alberto liked "mark it's only been like 3 months since we bought from henry"

Chris liked "mark it's only been like 3 months since we bought from henry"

Toodles liked "mark it's only been like 3 months since we bought from henry"

My Darling Sarah: so todd r u the new plug???

Jess emphasized "so todd r u the new plug???"

Alberto laughed at "so todd r u the new plus???"

Toodles: I thought I already bought you a plug?

My Darling Sarah questioned "I thought I already bought you a plug?"

Toodles: u know

Toodles: for ur butt

*You removed Toodles from the conversation.*

Jess: WTF

Grace disliked "for ur butt"

Alberto: Jesus

**Groupchat: STD Enthusiasts**

Frank: todd what the actual fuck

Alberto: That was the least funny thing

Frank: yeah dude fucking cringe

Marky Mark emphasized "yeah dude fucking cringe"

Chris: I have no dog in this fight, I thought it was funny

Chris: Fuck that bitch

Toodles loved "I have no dog in this fight, I thought it was funny"

Frank: u gotta apologize to sarah

Frank questioned "Fuck that bitch"

Toodles: oh jeez relax it was a fucking joke

*You removed Toodles from the conversation.*

Alberto: Aight frank ima add him back

Alberto: Cmon man

*Alberto added Toodles to the conversation.*

Frank took a deep breath. He exited out of the groupchat. He texted Todd.

**Toodles**

Frank: dude wtf

Toodles: sorry man lol didn't think you guys were still like a thing

Frank: that doesn't matter man, like u dont say that shit in front of girls

Frank: or TO girls

Toodles: ur the sexist for assuming their humor isn't as elevated as ours

Frank: butt plugs are elevated humor?

Frank: get a fucking grip

Toodles: no u get a fucking frip

Toodles: hrip

Toodles: grop

Toodles: GRip

Frank: are u drunk rn?

Toodles: fuck u dude

Frank texted Birdie.

**Birdie**

Frank: yo call todd i think he's drunk

Birdie: Okay

**Groupchat: Birdie's party**

Carissa: I feel like one of us should reach out to henry, let him know we're thinking about him

Chris: Lol i don't think anyone here gave a fuck about him unless they were buying from him

Marky Mark: Yeah idk if that'd be the best move

Jess emphasized "Lol i don't think anyone here gave a fuck about him unless they were buying from him"

Jess: god we suck

My Darling Sarah: im glad he's gone lol dude gave me the ducking creeps

Carissa: Don't say that! He just got expelled

Grace: I don't think he 'just' got expelled, probably happened a while ago

Grace: Like at graduation

Marky Mark emphasized "Like at graduation"

Chris: Lol sarah chill a kid just got expelled

Chris: It could just have easily been u

My Darling Sarah disliked "It could just have easily been u"

My Darling Sarah: chris stfu

My Darling Sarah: u don't even know me

My Darling Sarah: this groupchat is wack

**Groupchat: STD Enthusiasts**

Marky Mark: Frank what's up with sarah?

Frank: dude idk man

Marky Mark: U just gonna let her talk to chris like that?

Chris: Mark I can handle myself

Chris: Watch this

**Groupchat: Birdie's party**

Chris: Oh i know you sarah

Chris: I know enough

Chris: Remember when u asked me for an n-word pass freshman year?

Chris: I've known everything about you since then

**Groupchat: STD Enthusiasts**

Frank: chris yo what the actual fuck

Chris: What the actual fuck what?

Marky Mark: Guys cool it

Marky Mark: Fucking chill

Frank: chris dude why would u just bring up old dirt like that?

Chris disliked "chris dude why would u just bring up old dirt like that?"

Chris: Frank I love you man but sarah fucking sucks

Chris: Like what kind of bitch would fucking ever ask that?

Chris: U think Carissa would ever ask that?

Chris: Mark, u think grace would ever ask that?

Chris: I know damn well jess wouldn't ask that

Frank: thats cuz jess is indian of course she wouldn't ask that

**Groupchat: Birdie's party**

Alberto: yeah dude todd's hammered

Alberto: FUCK wrong chat

*Alberto added "Toodles" to the conversation.*

My Darling Sarah laughed at "yeah dude todd's hammered"

Carissa: TODD it's like 7 oh no

Jess disliked "yeah dude todd's hammered"

Grace: I think we should reconvene in a bit

Carissa loved "I think we should reconvene in a bit"

Carissa: Yeah things are weird

Toodles: AM not hmmerd

Alberto laughed at "AM not hmmerd"

Alberto laughed at "im glad he's gone lol dude gave me the ducking creeps"

**Groupchat: STD Enthusiasts**

Alberto named the conversation "AM not hmmerd"

**Groupchat: AM not hmmerd**

Marky Mark: Frank man u don't have to keep defending Sarah

Alberto: Yeah i'm all caught up now if what chris was saying is true then its all the more reason to forget her

Chris loved "Yeah i'm all caught up now if what chris was saying is true then its all the more reason to forget her"

Frank: I don't know why i'm still defending her

And it was true. Frank didn't know why he was still defending her. Well, that's not true. Frank knew damn well why he was still defending her. She was a piece of shit, a slut, a fucking racist even. But the way she held him. The way she cuddled. The way she took control. He couldn't lose that.

It was almost time for dinner. His mom was yelling at him from downstairs. Henry was really gone. Sarah was really gone. Although she wasn't. He still had to see her next year. Senior year.

So what, he'd made a mistake at Birdie's party. No one knew. Yet. Well, except her.

Except *her*.

*///Frank changed Sarah's contact from 'My Darling Sarah' to just 'Sarah' after dinner///*

# THE FIRST FRIDAY OF SUMMER. 9:20 PM.

———

Birdie emerged from the bathroom with white smoke trickling out of his mouth, whistling a tune.

Chris was finishing setting up the rack, and Todd had taken the liberty to begin pouring the beers. Mark loomed by his corner of the table, scrolling through something on his phone.

Birdie shuffled the ping-pong balls around in his pocket before pulling them out and rolling one to Chris, who had finished kissing his cups. He assumed his position on the right side of Todd.

"Cups look a little thick," he commented.

"Two beers, three beers, what's the difference?" Todd said as he crumpled a can and tossed it under the table.

Birdie had made it a point not to drink too much before the girls arrived. Now that the girls were here and sitting on the couch, sipping their seltzers and laughing at Frank, Birdie shrugged. "Three beers work for me."

He picked up the ball and splashed it in the water cup, feeling the weight in his hands. He flick-dried the ball, as though he were packing a tin, and remembered a funny story Mitch had once told him.

"Alright Albert," Chris began. Chris only called him "Albert" when they were competing. "Ready?"

Birdie bent his elbow, ready to shoot. Chris matched his form across the table.

"Eye...For...Eye," they said together, eyes locked. They shot like this to see which team started.

The balls collided mid-air, falling and bouncing chaotically on the linoleum floor.

~~~

"Stack him!" yelled Frank.

Sarah tried to stack her cup atop Mark's heaping stack of at least twenty cups, and knocked the whole thing over.

"Drink!"

Birdie resigned himself from the game to take another piss.

~~~

Now eight beers in, approximately (because it was hard to count when the cups weren't all the way full), Birdie busted out the deck of cards he and Maud had been playing with earlier. He figured the girls could use a break from the fast-paced drinking of stack-cup and knew that if he proposed running pong back he would have to wait a game or so until he got on the table. Todd had really blundered the last game, only hitting one cup and knocking over two of their own.

Two couches and two armchairs were misaligned around the coffee table. They could all fit, but it'd be a squeeze. He figured he oughtta secure an armchair now.

So he sat down and began to shuffle.

Carissa and Grace, giggling about something, came out of the bathroom and sat on the couch next to Birdie.

"Oooh, are we gonna play King's Cup?" Carissa asked. "Can I see your Juul?"

It was nice to see Carissa this eager, this excited, even if she was only one game of King's Cup away from throwing up.

"Yeah, I figured it'd be a good game for all of us to play." Birdie said, coolly. He felt nervous talking to Carissa, as if he had an impossible crush on her, or as if she had something stuck in her teeth and he was afraid of coming off as rude should he point it out.

"Frank, Sarah—You guys against me and Chris," Todd stammered loudly, leaning against the stove.

"We're gonna play King's Cup," Birdie announced. When he announced something, he knew people would listen.

"Nah, let's play pong. Then King's Cup," Sarah said. She was holding onto Frank's arm.

Grace was looking intently at something over Birdie's shoulder. At first, he thought she was looking at him, so he gave a cordial wave. When it didn't register, he turned to see what lie behind him.

Mark and Jess were outside, on the screened-in deck beyond the sliding doors, smoking cigarettes.

~~~

They'd all squeezed in, just as Birdie predicted, though Carissa was awkwardly forced to squat somewhere in between Birdie's armrest and the couch's armrest. It was her turn to draw a card.

The cards were laid out face-down in a circle around a can of White Claw, with about ten cards or so stuffed under the yet-unopened tab.

As she exerted her body to lean forward to draw a card, Birdie saw her bra underneath her loose-fitted tank top.

"It's a three!" she announced, nearly falling in between the two armrests. "Was that mean?"

"Oh, three!" Frank slapped the table. "That means—"

"Three for me," Birdie interrupted. He took Carissa's drink from the table and took three sips.

"Hey, those were supposed to be for her!" Frank contested.

Carissa didn't say anything, although Birdie was half-expecting a knowing, appreciative, soft, seductive whisper. Maybe even a mouthing of the word 'thanks.'

It was his turn now. He drew a card.

"Eight," he announced. "Pick a date."

He had to pick someone to 'date,' whereby from that point on whenever he drank, his date drank, and vice-versa. He expected Carissa to shift or motion to suggest discomfort. Again, her lack of action surprised him. He scanned the room. Grace was pushed up against the side of the couch by Carissa, and Frank and Sarah were cuddling-not-cuddling next to her, Todd sat in the armchair opposite him, and Chris, Jess, and Mark were sitting on the other couch.

He turned to his right and patted Mark on the shoulder. "Whaddaya say, buddy? Wanna go on a date with me?"

~~~

Birdie wasn't very good at pulling trig. He tried to shove his middle finger as far back down his throat as he could, to no avail. He just coughed and felt even more nauseous.

~~~

"Carissa, I'd really love to let you hit my Juul. I'd *really* love to. Fact of the matter is, however, it's on red. And the pod is low. And the rest of the pods are up in my bedroom in the main house, and I don't want to walk all the way up there right now."

~~~

"Balls back!"

~~~

Turned out Frank could, indeed, shotgun faster than Birdie. Why would he even challenge someone like Frank, who had at least twenty pounds on him?

At least Birdie didn't end up like Todd, who had to spit out most of the beer onto the linoleum on account of him thinking his mouth could hold more liquid than it evidently could.

~~~

Jess, lying on the couch, asked Birdie, "Why do you guys always say Chris is, like, well, *Chris?*"

Birdie had been on his phone playing some game, zoned out, for at least fifteen minutes. He started up, grabbed his beer, and yelled across the room, "Hey, Chris! Get over here!"

When Chris came over, he sat him down atop Jess' feet. "Now, Chris. The lovely Jess wanted know why Chris is *Chris*."

"Well, oh, well, you see, Chris is Chris is Chris, as in, *Chris*. You see? *Chrisssss...........*"

~~~

"I fucking *love* you guys," Todd was beaming with his arms around Birdie and Mark's shoulders. "Best roommates ever. I love your room, I love your friendship, I love you guys."

He smelt like puke.

~~~

Carissa was looking awfully cute, playing some hand game with Todd in the kitchen.

~~~

"Alright," and he was about to go off into a Birdieloquy, "like, okay, people these days, and I don't mean you, Mark, or Frank, or, like, alright maybe not people in the sense of all of *us*, right, but like, *people*, you know? Those intangible others we see every day and make fun of behind their backs. The NPCs, the CPUs, the sims, the bots, the more convincing evidence we're in a simulation, your Simon O'Malleys, what have you. Right? Like, people these days, those people, it's all just scrolling and yadda yadda and streaks and the bullshit and the shit that we do all the time but at least we, us, are sensible enough to notice it and comment on it, right? That's gotta be worth something."

~~~

Don't reckon Todd and Carissa would be a thing, right?

~~~

As it happened, as it was *wont* to happen, Birdie was one cup against Todd's one cup, in a one-v-one match of pong. So he straightened the cup in front of him out, pushed back against the edge of the table, centered.

So then, even though Birdie was pulling his shirt up and smacking his belly to distract his opponent, Todd did some sort of half-eyed hook shot from out deep and *sank* it. Splash. Now, he had another shot to ice it, of course. No chance he'd make it.

Well he tried that whole trick-shot half-trying shit again, and of course it flies far right and lands harmlessly on the ground. Was Carissa looking at him or Todd?

Birdie got a chance to redeem himself, a redemption shot. Well, two shots, since it was one-v-one. First shot he tried real casual-like, saying something like "and it take it to OT like *this*," but missed.

Was Carissa closer to him or Todd? Physically, on the side of the table. And who was she rooting for?

And where the hell was everyone else?

Jess and Chris were on the couch, cuddle-laughing and being all cute. Not a *thing*-thing, but a thing, for sure. Mark and Grace? Frank and Sarah?

Wait, no, *Mark and Grace?* No shot that was happening.

Shot. He had one shot left, to take it to overtime. He just had to hit the cup. Get serious this time, though not too serious. No joke shots, but God forbid he looked like he was trying.

He had to appear effortless, even though Carissa was scrolling.

"Ay, Birdie," from across the table. "Say you make it, right," and he was stammering and stammering and stammering. "I donwanna go into OT, so say you make it we call it a friendly draw?"

Grace came out from the kitchen with a granola bar in her hand. And it turns out Mark was over in the other corner charging his phone. Cool.

"Celeb shot?" Carissa asked, suddenly engaged.

Birdie caught himself smiling—uncool—and switched it up to a smirk. "Go for it," he said, handing her the wet ping pong ball.

He supposed that, while the ball was in the air, two realities branched off. One where she missed, and one where she made it. In the moment before the ball finished its arc, nearing the cup and certainly possibly going in (though certainly possibly rimming out), Birdie realized he didn't care whether he lost to Todd or not. His dick was lightly pressed against Carissa's thigh.

~~~

"Mark, things are cool with us, right man?" Birdie asked out back. Crickets. Literal crickets.

"Birdie, your cigarette's in the wrong way."

///Jess had asked Mark if he wanted to share a cigarette earlier as a means of explaining to him that Grace was, like, seriously super not over whatever it was between them.///

# FRIDAY, MAY 10TH, 2019. 8:20 PM.

———

They'd all gotten drunk about an hour earlier in his room, which was also Birdie's room. Mark, Birdie, Todd, Frank, Chris, Carissa, Sarah, and Jess. Well, actually, Chris didn't drink any. And Jess really only had a sip. It was Todd's—

"Jungle Juice, ladies and gentlemen. Assorted, blended, and curated by yours truly." Todd had clearly been taste-testing for a while before everyone showed up. "Brought to you by you, our listeners, and Mr. and Mrs. Marion."

Marion was Todd's last name, something Mark always forgot. 'Todd' was just so all-encompassing on its own.

But that was beside the point. The point, as Mark was realizing an hour or so after imbibing Todd's Jungle Juice, was that gin and rum should *not* be mixed with Baileys and whiskey and poured into an old Sprite bottle. Nor should Budweiser be used as a chaser.

It was a whole story, how Todd managed to sneak all his booze onto campus.

Aside from the hiccups, damn did it feel good to be buzzing. Mark let the spring breeze flow about his shorts and his t-shirt, rippling and soothing.

It had been tough getting the girls into his room. Normally, he and Birdie had to get verbal permission from whichever dorm parent (faculty member) was on duty that night. But because it was a Friday, everything was whack because the dorm parent wasn't on duty until 7:30. So at 7:00, when the girls showed up, no one was there to give an official Thumbs-Up. So he and Birdie just kind of led the girls to their room, unapproved.

And of course Frank was bugging out about it. Todd would've been too had he not already been pretty drunk. They'd all get in trouble for being together in a dorm room outside of faculty-approved parietals as it were; the alcohol (and Frank and Sarah and Birdie's Juuls, not to mention Chris and Todd's weed pens) would have surely gotten them at least suspended.

Mark had an exit strategy. If a faculty member knocked on the door and came in, he'd hide under his covers on the top bunk. None of his friends would rat him out if he didn't get caught.

So they all took turns swigging from Todd's collection of Sprite bottles, chasing it down with warm beer. The best part was that for all of Mark's worrying, no faculty member ever knocked on their door, and at 7:25, when they left, there wasn't a faculty member even in the lobby.

"We could totally get away with this more often," Birdie said as he tied a sweater to his waist in the foyer.

"That's what everyone thinks before they get caught," Mark replied. This was fun, and would be fun if they did it again, but it was definitely a once-a-semester sort of shindig. Otherwise, the novelty was gone. Half the fun was totally just from the threat of getting caught, the thrill of doing something new.

On the walk to the Student Center, where they kind of just decided to go (without Mark's input), Birdie explained the situation. "So, Frank and Sarah are totally gonna dip off to hook up, which Todd is so-so about. At least he was so-so earlier. He doesn't seem to give a fuck now. And Chris, well, Jess has got it *bad* for him."

"For Chris?"

"For Chris, yes. So we'll see. Maybe Chris will surprise us."

Chris had never, in his life, kissed a girl. He was handsome and relatively charming but, as Chris put it, "the opportunity just hadn't presented itself."

So here were eight seventeen-year-olds walking at quite the clip, loaded up with booze, on their way to purchase chicken fingers from the café at their boarding school's Student

Center. Mark knew it was ridiculous, but it felt good to be doing something out of the ordinary.

Hell, maybe it was the booze or the company or the atmosphere or *what*, but he hadn't felt weird at all that night. No slips "into the void," as Birdie referred to Mark's episodes.

When they got to the Student Center they were all a bit bummed to find it empty.

"I can't believe it's dead in here," Frank said, running his hand over his face. They'd all squeezed into a booth. Well, Mark had to pull up a chair. But at least he was the head of the table.

"Ha-ha, *bummer dude*." Todd could hardly sit up straight, but his impression of Sean Penn in *Fast Times at Ridgemont High* was still spot-on. "Oh, and dude," Todd whispered to Mark, "*how the fuck could I, like, seriously just lose a pocket pussy?*"

Carissa, meanwhile, was looking fucking gorgeous and it was clear she hadn't put in any effort whatsoever. Gray St. D's sweatpants, a tie-dye t-shirt, messy hair. Her eyes.

Grace had asked Mark who he thought the prettiest girl in their grade was, about a year ago. After answering "Grace" five times, and getting punched in the shoulder five times, Mark yielded that it'd have to be Carissa. "But you're obviously gorgeous too, hon."

*Is Sarah giving Frank a handjob under the table?*

Probably not, but they were getting awfully familiar. They'd hooked up what, like six times over three years?

Birdie, Todd, and Chris had all obviously smoked prior. They were debating whether they'd rather fight five Dr. Andlers or one Mr. Fenton. (Dr. Andler was a feisty woman in her mid-fifties who hardly weighed a hundred pounds; Mr. Fenton evened out the scale at about five Dr. Andlers).

Mark heard himself breathing through his nose. That usually was a terrifying thing, an insufferable thing. But it just then reminded him of his existence, his energy. Everything was happening fast.

*Yeah, I'm definitely drunk.*

Oh, and then Frank and Chris started to arm-wrestle. Definitely attracting too much negative attention to themselves. What if a faculty roamer walked by?

Poor Jess. She'd been desperately laughing along to just about every argument Chris made about how he could fend off five Dr. Andlers with his four limbs. And now, she was on her phone, reeling from the lack of recognition.

Chris beat Frank quite handily the first round, but in the rematch Frank was putting up a solid fight.

Birdie put his two hands over the arm-wrestlers' locked fist. "Stop," he said. "You guys…," he looked around, and lowered his voice: "You guys are being too loud. Do you want to get caught?"

"I uh, well, catch me if you can. Good movie, no?" Todd muttered.

*Oh boy.*

Sarah was resting her head against Frank's shoulder, eyes closed. Jess put her phone on the table face-down.

"Hey, Mark," Carissa whispered, tugging at the bottom of his shirt. "Can I talk to you?"

Well, here was a welcome surprise. Could he afford to leave? Or worse, if he left, would Birdie or Todd follow? Birdie would take care of Todd, no doubt. Birdie seemed fine. And Frank, well he and Sarah would be inside of each other soon enough. *Jesus, did I really just say that in my head?* Who knew about Chris and Jess?

"Yeah," Mark managed, realizing he'd left Carissa hanging. "Let's, uh, let's go."

It wasn't until they exited the Student Center with no trail that Mark was confident they wouldn't be followed. It only took a couple steps after that for him to wonder if Carissa wanted to hook up.

"So, what's up?" he asked. She was several paces in front of him, leading him back toward the dorms.

She must not have heard. It was fine to walk in silence, though. He was getting hot in the Student Center, perspiring on the forehead and clammy in the hands, so the fresh air felt nice. His hands swooshed by his sides with every step.

Carissa had achieved good separation by the time they passed the chapel. The lights from the chapel illuminated her figure, walking as if on a tight rope on the grass in front of him.

"Carissa!" Mark said, loud enough for her to hear. "Don't do that!"

She stopped administering herself a sobriety test and, presumably satisfied with the results, began to sprint toward the pond.

Mark, who at this point was rocking a solid half-chub, tucked his business into his waistband. He had no choice but to follow her.

They probably weren't going to hook up tonight. Or any night. Why had he even thought she'd go for him? It didn't make any sense. He was walking awkwardly fast, such that it'd be easier if he just bust into a light jog.

Up ahead Carissa had disappeared in the darkness by the waterfront.

*It's good to be drunk.* How many times was he going to think that? But really, it was. It calmed him. He didn't have to worry about a toe-twitch or a slip. Usually, just thinking about such things brought them on; when he was drunk, Mark could look at his condition and analyze it, without the fear of succumbing to it. Perhaps he could always do this; more likely it was the alcohol numbing his body.

It was easy to see why Todd was such a big fan of this stuff. Burned like Hell going down, but it had kept Mark warm inside ever since.

Cause it was real shame, not being able to smoke weed anymore. He'd tried it a couple of times after the trip, but it just made him re-enter that horrible headspace. Birdie was convinced Mark was just in his own head. And Birdie was always right. But what the fuck was he supposed to do? Just get out of his own head?

Now that he was closer he could make out Carissa, perched up on the Big Rock. It was called so because it was a big rock by the pond. Clever.

"Howdy!" Carissa exclaimed, waving at Mark.

He climbed up to sit next to her.

The view wasn't all that much: just soccer fields behind the chapel and the distant roar of cars. Not too many cars on the road at night, though.

"What's up?" Mark asked.

Carissa didn't respond. The crickets around the pond chirped. *Wow.*

So they just sat in silence, both breathing heavily. Without being obvious, Mark turned his head toward Carissa's. Her head was rolled back, her gaze star-ward. Unclear if her eyes were open.

"Y'know, we don't talk much," she finally said, bringing her head back to look at Mark. "You and I never really hang out."

"I guess, yeah." Is that why he was out here? The prep-school equivalent of a drunken 'let's get coffee tomorrow and catch up,' only to go months again without talking? Honestly, he was all for it. He'd always wanted to get closer to Carissa. Given the state she was in now, however, this probably wasn't the start of a close friendship.

She burped. "Excuse me," she said. She jolted up.

"Actually, that's not true," Mark said. "We've hung out before."

"Really? When?"

"About a month back, in the woods. What was it, Patriots Day?"

Carissa lightly punched his arm and smiled. "I dunno why I was fucking with you, I remember that. I just wanted to make sure you remembered that too."

"Yeah, that was Patriots Day," Mark began, verbalizing his recollection as it came to him. "Birdie wanted to bike into town but the weather was shitty...Todd and Frank got high in the morning and were catapulting Goldfish at Sarah with their spoons. And then, oh wait, Birdie and I went on a walk to the fields, something he had to tell me—"

*Oh, fuck.*

Carissa sniffled.

"He had to tell me, uhh…well that was the day after Maury—"

"So you knew?" Carissa said. He could practically hear the tears welling in her eyes.

"I didn't want to say anything." It was true. Mark had gone for his own walk after Birdie told him what had happened, not necessarily because he was so deeply affected by it, but because he'd been meaning to go for a walk anyway. It had stopped raining, and he found a nice large stump on the cross-country course that was dry enough to sit on, and posted up for a bit.

"You didn't say anything about it," Carissa said.

"What was there to say?" It was true. He'd thought about saying something like, 'oh I'm so sorry,' but what would that accomplish? If anything, all it would have done was let Carissa know that people on campus had already found out.

"How did you find out so soon?" she asked. From the sound of it, she'd swallowed her tears. She seemed desperate, as if this had been burning in her mind for far too long.

"Well, Birdie found out first. His friend Carl, at Harvard, well *he* knew. I guess it spread quick around campus. Birdie and Carl have known each other for years, family friends. Carl went to Groton."

Carissa didn't say anything. It was unclear if she was anticipating more, or if she was just processing what she'd heard.

"And so Carl heard about a St. D's kid at Harvard getting blackout drunk and pushing his girlfriend down a flight of stairs, and, well..."

He expected tears, but heard none. He supposed the well had run dry after a month.

"I hate him so much," Carissa said instead.

"Carissa, he was blackout drunk—"

"No!" Carissa collected herself. "That's not an excuse."

"I mean, I hear where you're coming from. But believe me, as someone who's been blackout drunk, it's like you don't have control over your actions." He'd never been blackout, but that was what Todd said it was like. "Look, you can blame Maury, or Alex, all you want. And he definitely deserves most of the blame. But what about his friends, huh? His friends he was with? The ones that let him go into that stairwell with his girlfriend, knowing full well how fucked up he was?"

This wasn't something Mark had thought about before. At this point, the words were coming out faster than he could think them.

"Yeah, what great friends, huh? Let the blackout kid go off on his own with his equally drunk girlfriend. They'll surely be okay! And you know what? When we finally realized that we should check on them, and we see they're fighting, let's just walk away! Let them deal with it! And when we come back in five minutes, and Maury's holding his girlfriend's bloody head in his hands two flights down crying out 'I'm sorry! I'm sorry!' let's fucking *ask if everything's alright. And when he yells 'go away,' *why don't you just fuck off.*"

He turned to meet her gaze. It'd been a long time since he looked at a girl in the eyes this intimately.

"Mark—"

"Great fucking friends they are!"

"Mark—"

"Maury's life wouldn't be over, neither would that poor girl's…"

"Mark!"

"What!?"

"You're crying."

And he was. He wiped both the tears away. Fuck, it was nice to cry. He imagined the thought of crying in front of someone like Carissa Moraine to be humiliating, or pathetic, but it was just so…pure. Cathartic.

God, he felt good. He laughed.

"Mark, I know what happened to you," Carissa said, smiling. They had locked eyes again, seeing each other.

Mark swatted a mosquito from his face too hard. "Ow," he said with a smile.

"Did you hear me? I said—"

"I heard you. How do you know?"

Mark hadn't assumed it was the best kept secret on campus that his mind was broken. Not that everyone would find out and whisper about it, or anything. Just that some of his behavior around the people he spent the most time with had to be explained eventually.

"Well, Grace told me," she said.

Mark broke eye contact. "How the hell did Grace know?"

"Birdie. As soon as you re-tripped the first time, which was after he found out you two split, he met with her and asked what had happened. He scared her."

Perhaps Mark was too hard on Birdie. "Wait, he scared her?"

"Yeah, he was yelling something like, '*you broke my best friend!*'"

Mark sighed, the kind that sounds like a laugh.

"Mark, Maury had shitty friends. But you don't."

"Well, have you seen Frank's impression of—"

Carissa put her finger up to his mouth to shush him. He smiled. He hadn't been touched by a girl at school since Grace, three months ago.

"Alex shouldn't have drank so much. It doesn't matter that he was blackout, or abandoned by his friends…he had the capacity to hurt someone that badly, deep down within him. The alcohol only brought that out."

"Carissa, with all due respect, that's bullshit."

"Oh really? Listen to me, Mark. You should've told your friends Grace broke up with you. Then they wouldn't have let you trip on shrooms in the first place."

"What does that have to do with—"

"*Listen.* But even if you picked a different time, or a different place, under different circumstances, we both know you would've had a bad trip regardless."

"What? No." *What the fuck?* "Shut the fuck up. You don't know shit about me."

"Grace had told me—"

"Oh, so Grace has told you what, exactly?"

He didn't even want to yell. He wanted to cry. He wanted to hear Carissa tell him everything about him. He wanted to curl up into a ball.

"Mark, you're yelling."

"So what I'm yelling?"

"Calm down, Mark. Listen to me. I'm just gonna say what I have to say, and then you can react."

*Please don't stop talking.*

"Mark, you are an incredibly anxious, fucked up, emotionally suppressed mess," she said, slowly. "And you never should have faced yourself under the influence of psychedelics before sorting all of that out."

Obviously. He'd known it ever since the trip. Grace was just a beautiful, easy scapegoat.

"Let me get this straight," Mark began in a defensive tone. "Are you trying to equate me to your murderous older brother in this therapy session? Because if so, you shouldn't have picked an awfully dark place near a body of water."

She laughed, luckily.

"Grace misses being with you, but trust me, she doesn't miss dealing with all your bullshit."

"Bullshit that I assume you're privy to, Ms. Moraine?"

Where he expected a laugh, he was met with a silence.

"I can't stand the way people see me," she said after a moment or so.

"You're beautiful, funny, and cool as fuck. What am I missing?" Mark said. Obviously they weren't going to hook up after pouring their souls out. That didn't mean he couldn't flatter her.

"I'm not Carissa Moraine anymore. Maybe I never really was. But now it's a done-deal: I'm Alex Moraine's Little Sister. My life doesn't even pass the Bechdel test anymore."

"Bullshit. If you're just 'Alex Moraine's Little Sister,' then I'm just 'Birdie Fayter's Sidekick.'"

"At least people are nice to you because of it," Carissa joked. "People avoid me as if *I* did it."

"Yeah, that sucks. But it also sucked freshman year when people would be all nice to me just to get closer to Birdie."

Carissa burst out laughing. It was unclear if it was a cathartic "look at us" laugh, or the booze, or something else. Whatever it was, she had caught a bad case of the giggles.

Mark checked his phone. No texts, but it was already 10:17. It fucking sucked that in thirteen minutes they all had to be back in their dorms. It was a Friday night! He was sitting outside, buzzed, next to a beautiful woman, spilling their guts out for each other! He could do this all night!

Carissa eventually quieted down, not before letting another one of their numbered minutes pass by.

"Wanna tell me what's so funny?" Mark asked.

"You're gonna hate me," Carissa said, wiping a tear from her eye. "But do you think I have a chance at getting with Birdie?"

How could he be mad? He knew Carissa had the hots for Birdie. And it's not like he was shitting on Birdie, or anything.

"Wait," Mark wagged his finger. "Was this all an elaborate ruse to get closer to me and transitively get closer to—"

Carissa punched Mark hard on the shoulder.

"Ow!"

"Of course this was all real! I wasn't even thinking about Birdie until you brought him up."

"Well either way, I'm sorry for fucking up your date." Mark sighed. "I don't know why he hasn't asked you out again."

"It's Birdie, who knows why he does anything."

"I heard my name!" shouted Birdie, from the sidewalk below.

Of fucking course. That kid had perfect timing whenever he showed up. Todd was next to him, leaning against a tree.

"Hey, Birdie." Mark said. "Whatcha been up to?"

"Well," Birdie said, and breathed in deep. He was gonna get this all out in one breath. "Chris beat Frank in about eight arm-wrestles, and then Sarah beat Todd, so then Frank picked up Sarah, and they ran off together, and then Chris and Jess were just, like, holding each other's' hands and staring into each other's eyes, so Todd and I dipped off to go shoot some hoops in the gym but Todd's shot was so atrociously bad that I figured if any roamer were to come in and see the absolute smackdown I was laying on Todd they would immediately suspect something was up because let's face it Todd usually has my number when it comes to hoops, so then we walked a bit around campus and heckled some couples hooking up and now we're here." He gasped. "Ain't that right, buddy?"

"Yeah, Steph Curry." Todd muttered. His state clearly hadn't improved.

"So help us settle a bet. Did you two hook up?" Birdie was still winded.

"What? No!" Mark and Carissa said together.

"It's almost time to go back," Carissa stated. She stood up and was wrapping her sweater around her waist. Her dorm was in between the Big Rock and Lang.

"Yo, Todd, T-Bone," Mark teased. He hopped down and helped Carissa off the rock. "Todd, what were you saying the other day about being faster than me?"

"Oh, I kick your *ass*, Duplessis!" Todd said, running in place.

"Alright, Todd. To the AC and back to Lang. Ready! Set!" Mark announced. He turned back to Carissa and winked.

"Wait! Wait! I oughta tie my shoe!" Todd complained.

"Hey, Birdie, why don't you walk Carissa back to her dorm?" Mark suggested, and then winked again.

*Damn, I'm really fucking good at winking.*

Standing up after sitting down for so long reawakened the booze which had grown dormant in his belly. "I feel good, Todd, your ass is grass!"

"Go!" Todd yelled, and took off toward the AC.

Mark looked back at Carissa, who smiled, and then at Birdie, who slapped him on the ass and told him to run. So he bolted. Full speed. Fastest he'd run in months. Years. His whole life. Speeding, whirring across the grass, turning around the lamp post, barely in control. Let loose, unchained. Free.

*///Mark jacked off that night and blew a load so big that it got in his eye. The next day, he accused Todd of farting on his pillow to explain why his eye was so red. Todd denied this vehemently, but had no alibi on account of blacking out.///*

# THE SNOW DAY.
# 12:30 PM.

---

It should've been her little brother Alex out there shoveling snow, not Grace.

She was six years older than Alex, and thus didn't have any interest in really getting to know him. While he was inside playing Fortnite in the basement, warm and carefree, she was out here busting her ass clearing the freshly fallen snow from their horrendously long driveway.

She was eleven when her dad first made her shovel the driveway. Alex had turned eleven last week.

It had been about an hour since she'd strapped on her snow boots and bundled up to start shoveling. Her dad hadn't even asked her to do it. Over breakfast he just stated, "So, Grace, it's stopped snowing."

It was all fucking bullshit. All of it. Everything. At least she didn't have to go to school today and see Mark. Not that she regretted her decision. It was, well, about time. He'd said, *Is two and a half years really, like, an anniversary though?* Thank God he'd said it, honestly. It gave her a reason to explode at him.

Of course, then he went into defense mode. And when he realized that she was going to break up with him, he went into panic mode.

That son of a bitch made it hard. Hard to tell if he was being genuine, hard to tell if he really wanted to be in the relationship, hard to tell if he was trying to guilt her into submission. So it was hard to break up with him. Harder than it should have been. Harder than the ice underneath all of the snow that she had to smash with the shovel to break up.

But it still wouldn't break. The plastic shovel wasn't doing the trick. She needed the metal shovel. But maybe if she just hit it at the right angle, hard enough. Harder. Two hands gripping the handle, really putting all of her weight into each blow.

She smashed the shovel into broken bits of green plastic, til there was nothing but a wooden rod in her hands.

She was breathing heavily now, breath floating in front of her, mocking her. And someone was calling her, not that she could answer the phone now anyway. It was in the pocket of her sweatpants, which were underneath her snow pants.

Grace fell to the ground, landing on a cushion of snow. She'd meant to gracefully sit down, but slipped on the ice she'd been trying to break up.

Snow brushed up against her ears as she lay down on her back. Maybe her parents would see her like this and think she hurt herself on the ice, that she was unconscious. They'd rush out, *Grace! Grace!*, and call for paramedics. A helicopter would fly overhead with a big, red cross on it, and two doctors would descend on a ladder to hoist her up. They'd be muscular and impossibly good-looking, like on TV. And she'd feel weightless in their arms.

Her phone rang again. Maybe it was Mark. *We're not, like, really broken up, right?* And then what would she say? *Yes.* Only she might not. Not that she didn't want to still be broken up, but hearing him so defeated and helpless, maybe she'd cave. She could always break up with him again, but that'd be a nuisance.

Her parents never came out, never mind the hunky heli-doctors. She got up herself, nearly slipping on the ice again. That would have been fucking hilarious, wouldn't it have? She laughed and laughed and laughed as she walked to the garage.

Inside, she stripped off her winter coat and unfastened her boots and took off her snow pants.

Three missed calls from Carissa Moraine.

She tried to call her back, fingers red and stiff, but the touch-ID wasn't working and she couldn't bring up the passcode page.

*I never asked them to take away the home button.*

Luckily, amidst her struggles, Carissa rang her again.

"Hello?" Grace said, struggling to get a firm grasp on her phone as she brought it to her ear.

"Why are you out of breath?" asked the cheery voice on the other end.

Grace briefly explained what she was up to, minus destroying the shovel and heli-doctor fantasy.

"Yuck, shoveling sucks. Luckily Alex is still home on winter break. He's been out shoveling for over an hour."

Even as she got to know Carissa and her family better, it was still surprising to hear her call Maury 'Alex.' Sure, Carissa would never call her brother the nickname he had based off of their last name. But he'd always been Maury to Grace. Something about the two of them both having brothers named Alex also didn't feel right, especially when Alex Martin was an infantile piece of shit and Alex Moraine was a living god.

"Are you still there?" Carissa asked.

"Yeah, sorry, it's just I didn't know who you were talking about, *hahaha.* I wish I was in college. Their breaks are so long!"

Even though they'd been over to each other's houses and met each other's families and hung out regularly now, Grace still worried she sometimes came across as eager. Which was dumb. Carissa and Grace naturally hit it off. And it wasn't like Grace was clout-chasing or anything. She didn't need that. It was just hard to shake the Carissa of freshman and sophomore years, or her perception of Carissa then, to her friend Carissa now.

"Anyway, Grace, I have the exciting news. Birdie asked me on a date today!"

She never really saw what Carissa saw in Birdie. Probably because Carissa hadn't spent two years dating his roommate. No, two-and-a-half years.

Maybe two-and-a-half years wasn't a real anniversary after all.

Grace nevertheless expressed sympathetic excitement with a giddy "Eeeeeee!!" which she hated herself for doing.

"So it's gonna be a double-date, right. Like, me and Birdie, and then Todd and Sarah."

"I thought Sarah was with Frank?"

"Eh, together, not-together, hooking up sometimes. Although I guess it's been a while since they hooked up. And you know Todd, it's probably all just a joke to get Frank upset."

"Why would Sarah agree to go out with Todd?"

"Todd's got booze and can get Juul pods. So it's like, a tit-for-tat thing. And anyway, Sarah always thought Todd was kinda funny."

"Yeah, Todd's hilarious." Grace hated Todd's humor.

"Annnyyyywaaayyy I was hoping you and Mark could join us! I could really use some support tonight."

So Mark hadn't told anyone that she broke up with him? Maybe he really didn't think they were broken up.

"Uh, I don't know…"

"Oh please, Grace! It'll be so much fun!"

She tried to say *we broke up*, but somehow couldn't get the words out. Like, physically couldn't say it.

"Hello?"

Seriously, it was weird. She couldn't say it. It wasn't an emotional thing, it wasn't a never-said-it-out-loud-and-thus-never-made-it-real thing, or maybe it was. It just didn't sound right in her head.

"Grace?"

*We broke up.* Nope, the words didn't work. Stunned by her failure to utter those three simple words, her mouth hung open, frozen.

"Are you still there?"

But then it came. Not those words, but something else.

"I broke up with that son of a bitch last night," she said and smiled.

*///It cost $35 to replace the shovel. Mr. Martin, four weeks later after another snowstorm, found an extra shovel hidden behind two trashcans in the garage. Having just purchased a brand new shovel, and having struggled with an emerging case of erectile dysfunction for the past several weeks, Mr. Martin smashed the new shovel to bits on the concrete floor of the garage.///*

# WEDNESDAY, NOVEMBER 7TH, 2018. 3:11 PM.

---

Wednesdays were usually game day. Game day for Todd meant getting high in the showers before kickoff, during halftime, and after the game. Every now and then he'd run a streak or a slant or curl, but he could count the number of times on one hand that star freshman QB Matt Lester threw the ball in his direction.

Whenever he tried to do so he made a fist, which he sometimes shook in anger.

This Wednesday, however, their scheduled football match at the prestigious Xavier Academy had been cancelled on account of every senior and most of the juniors on the Xavier football team being suspended from the school on charges of hazing, cheating, and consuming chewing tobacco on the bus.

*Dip.* Copenhagen Long Cut Wintergreen smokeless tobacco. Mitch offered him some now.

They were in Mitch's car. He was also a junior on the football team, cornerback and punter.

"I've never packed a lip before," Todd admitted.

Mitch was a fine enough guy, maybe a bit slow in the head. Wasn't very good at football, but loved hitting people. As a result, he got hit back. A lot.

"What kind of defensive player takes as many hits to the head as you?" Coach Stevens would ask Mitch on the sidelines.

"Not so much," Mitch would answer, once pulled from the game after falling unconscious when a frustrated receiver had tackled *him* to the ground.

Anyway, Todd was wondering whether or not he wanted to try it out. Dip. It looked pretty fucking nasty, and Mitch looked particularly repulsive with his fat lip, holding a repurposed Gatorade bottle between his legs as a spittoon.

*Should he be driving like this?*

"It's easy, T-Bone," Mitch said and spat. "Alls you do is open up the tin with your nails, pinch off some, and stick it in your lip like this." Mitch took his hands off the wheel to pull down his lip, revealing a dark wad of saliva and tobacco.

"Focus on the road, man. I've got this."

Todd decided he'd pack a small lip, a 'skittle' as Mitch called it. The tin was deceivingly hard to get open.

"You gotta use your thumbs," Mitch suggested.

The recognition that he was struggling somehow made it even harder, not to mention the pang of embarrassment Todd felt. This wasn't his zone, this hick shit.

He finally got it open and quickly tried to pinch off the tiniest amount Mitch would allow him to take. That is, until Mitch interrupted, "Oh wait, I'm retarded. You gotta pack it first so it's not all loose like that."

"How do I pack it?" Todd asked. If it weren't for the fact that Mitch was unwittingly doing him a huge favor, he'd have thrown the tin out the window.

"Like, you know, *this,*" Mitch mimicked the motion of packing a tin—thumb pressed against middle finger, whipped downward, index finger crashed against the imaginary tin with an audible *smack.*

So he figured he'd try it. If he fucked it up, hopefully Mitch would just drop it. He put the lid back on, held the tin using only his thumb and middle finger, and whipped it downward.

Only Todd hadn't secured the lid properly. He didn't know that the lid was only securely fastened after an audible *pop.* So instead of packing the tobacco tighter within the tin, he inadvertently launched the tobacco out over the entire car.

"Jesus fuck!" Mitch exclaimed. He reached down for his spittoon to spit.

Did Mitch always salivate when he was startled?

It was pretty fucking hilarious, honestly. There hadn't been too much left in the tin anyway. Mitch's face, however, looked like Todd had killed his firstborn son or something.

"Get the fuck out of my car," Mitch demanded after they pulled over.

Todd had been picking up as much of the tobacco as he could, although admittedly he knew it was a futile effort. Little brown shards were in every crevice and crack in the cushions and doors, the dashboard, even the glove compartment. Some had gotten in Mitch's blond hair, too, but it probably wasn't worth mentioning to him.

They were probably two miles off campus.

"Seriously?" Todd asked.

"Get out!"

So that was that, then. Another plan foiled. It had been a solid plan, too. Foolproof. More importantly, detection-proof.

Todd began the trek back to campus defeated, but with high spirits. At least he didn't have to sit on a bus for two hours both ways to Xavier and back. At least Mitch would stop asking him to hang out. At least he had a plan.

It was hard not to crack up at the thought of all that tobacco flying everywhere.

"Man, that was fucking hysterical," he whispered to himself. With no sidewalk on the road, he was doing his best to tip-toe in between the white line of the road and the steep drop-off into dirt and shrubs.

"I talk to myself," he said. "I bet Birdie does too."

A car zipped by a bit too close. The bumper stickers on the car were all St. D's.

"Can't you see I'm walking here?"

Someone was calling him. Birdie. His contact name in Todd's phone was "Birdo McFuckface."

"Yello."

"Ay, yo, Todder, where you at?"

Something about *walking back to campus* didn't feel right. If anyone didn't need to know the reason why Mitch had abandoned him, it was Birdie.

"You know, just chillin'."

"Didn't you say you were tryna get into town for that secret mission? Me and the love birds are—" someone interrupted him. Laughter exploded from the other end of the phone. "Sorry, me and Mark and his lovely girlfriend Grace are driving into town too."

Todd hung up the phone. Up ahead, Grace's unmistakable neon green Kia Soul was already slowing down.

The car pulled over on the other side of the road. Birdie rolled down his window and yelled, "Need a ride, stranger? We'll take you as far as downtown, but you're gonna have to put those sweet lips to use if you want to get any farther!"

It took a bit of convincing to get Grace to help Todd realize his plan. Most of the heavy-lifting on the negotiations came from Birdie, who had his own interests vested heavily in the operation's success. Birdie got Grace to agree to pick them up from the liquor store in exchange for one all-expenses paid date with Mark.

Mark, who was sitting shotgun, didn't say much.

The grocery store was the easy part. Todd got what he needed (two twelve-packs of Coca-Cola, and a twelve-pack of Barq's Root Beer) and brought those back to the car while Grace and Mark shopped. He and Birdie then unloaded all of the cans into Todd's backpack.

Now equipped with three empty cardboard boxes with soda labels on them, and a backpack drooping to his ass with weight, they walked the .4 miles to Dawson's Liquors.

"You feeling good?" Birdie asked.

This was the hard part. Todd had used his fake several times before, to buy Juul pods at easy gas stations, but he'd never used it to buy booze.

"Well," he replied, "I've gotta find out at some point if this thing works. Might as well be today."

Birdie waited outside, holding the cardboard boxes. Todd walked through the automatic glass doors.

He looked old enough, sure. Baseball cap, button down shirt, jeans. Good shoes, too. Not sneakers. Hell, he was even wearing fancy socks, as if that was something the cashier would notice. It all made him *feel* adult—college, leisurely beers for the weekend. He lives in Philly, goes to Penn State. They're all out for Thanksgiving break right now. Yeah, he knows, it starts super early. That's why he's out here, at his friend's house. All the way out here in MA. And, by the way, what *is* the legal age for tobacco out here anyway?

The conversation rushed through Todd's head as it had a thousand times over. A suave, twenty-two-year-old Penn State kid. Senior year of college. He had even picked out his major, psychology. In case they asked.

And he hadn't been in Philly long, in case the cashier knew Philly well. No, his parents had just moved out there when he enrolled at Penn State. Originally from Des Moines. No shot the cashier knew Des Moines.

And his friend, the one from Penn State, lived nearby. Oh, he didn't know. Maybe Oak Street? Couldn't remember. He was pretty sure. Though it sure was pretty out here.

These hypothetical conversations, of which none were sure to ever actually happen, made Todd confident. He wasn't Todd Marion, seventeen, from Attleboro MA. He was Todd Marrone, twenty-two, from Philly by way of Des Moines.

He had to get the right beer, that was key. Twenty-four Budweisers and twelve Coors Light. All cans. Otherwise the colors wouldn't match. Unfortunately, they only sold thirty-racks of Budweiser cans, the twelve-packs were bottles. So he grabbed a thirty-rack of Budweiser clumsily from the cooler, trying to pick it up by the handle and finesse it out in one swift motion. He banged the case loudly against the ledge of its shelf in the cooler.

He grabbed the twelve-pack of Coors Light cans with considerably more grace and attention.

The thirty-rack in his left hand (compared to the twelve-pack in his right) made him lean awkwardly as he walked to the counter.

So here's how Todd told the story to Birdie, when they began unloading the cans into the cardboard boxes with soda labels:

"She was like, *Oh, Philly? What are you doin' out here?* And I told her, 'Oh I'm just visiting a friend from college. You know Penn State lets out too early for Thanksgiving break,' which I don't even know is true by the way. So she's like, *You go to*

*Penn State?* And of course I'm like 'Yeah.' So then she asks me, and you're not gonna believe this, she says *Do you know my daughter, Ellen? She'd probably be in your grade.* So I say 'I know a couple of Ellens, what's her last name?' And she says *Flenser,* and I'm like, 'Shut up! You're Ellen Flenser's mom!' And then we chat about Ellen, and I tell her I don't know her too well, but we've got mutual friends and that she should tell her daughter that I send my regards, and then I wished her and her family a happy Thanksgiving."

Only what really happened was nothing; total buildup, anticipation, for the cashier to just scan the ID. Which of course got approved, the new Chinese fake IDs pass scanners.

They put the silver Coors Light into the Barq's and the red Budweisers into the Coca-Cola.

"Hey, we've got six beers left over," Birdie commented. "And look, Grace and Mark are pulling in."

That damn neon green beacon.

"Yeah, I figure you, me, and Mark can split 'em on the drive back to campus," Todd said, cracking open one of the extra Buds.

Only Grace wouldn't let Mark have any, him sitting shotgun and all. *What if a cop sees you? Or worse, a faculty member!*

So Todd and Birdie chugged three beers in the backseat throughout the eight-minute drive back to campus, belching and laughing in victory.

Grace never said a word. Nor did Mark. Their loss.

And the best part, out of all of it, was that when Todd and Birdie walked back to the dorm carrying their haul, they were stopped by the Dean of Students, Mr. Welsh. Of course, it didn't look suspicious at all, just some students carrying soda back to their room from town. Mr. Welsh just wanted to comment on how warm it was for November. But little did he know, Todd (and by extension Birdie) had kicked his administrative ass.

///*Grace, who had received two C's on important tests that week and had overheard a heated argument between her parents over financial aid the night before, reamed into Mark for having degenerate friends who don't consider anyone other than themselves after dropping Todd and Birdie off at campus.*///

# SIX

# THE FIRST DAY OF SCHOOL. 8:08 PM.

———

The only junior Carissa ever really knew when she was a freshman was her older brother and a couple of his buddies she'd met at their house before. In her freshman-year dorm, the junior girls all had their own floor. Carissa barely saw them, aside from during dorm meetings. Not that Carissa thought she'd really hit it off with them or anything. They were all friends because of their shared passion for academics and theater, two things Carissa did not find particularly exciting. Still, it was strange to every so often see one of the junior girls in her dorm and not even know what her name was.

Now Carissa had the opportunity to be that mysterious and nameless junior girl. Sarah, Jess, Tish, Em, and her…they could all become *that* group. Instead of academics and theater, they'd be united in squash and good looks. God, why was she thinking like that? Sarah didn't even play squash. Not to mention Em's looks.

*There I go again.*

She wanted to crush this year after what had been an enjoyable if not dull sophomore year. She wanted to do better in her classes, especially math, because college applications were right around the corner. She wanted to destroy the SATs on her first try. She wanted to use the fall as a time to really get in great shape (she believed she'd gone a bit squishy over the summer). Squash season was right around the corner. She wanted to make new friends, try new things. She wanted to finally hook up with someone at school, now that her older brother was off to college and could no longer intimidate the boys in her grade. She wanted to run for Student Senate, get involved with the community, boost her extracurriculars. College applications were right around the corner.

But she also didn't want to be *that* girl, the one who did it all. The one who doesn't have time for the goofing off and the chilling because she has too much on her plate. The one who focuses too much on the college applications, which were right around the corner...

And she certainly didn't want to be *that* junior girl the freshmen in her dorm couldn't remember the name of. She'd make sure of that tonight.

"Hey, Sarah, why don't we invite some of the freshman up to our room?" Carissa asked, turning to face her roommate. They were lying next to each other in Sarah's bed, sharing pictures from their summers.

"I got a glimpse of them last night during the dorm meeting. They look like a bunch of losers," Sarah said, eyes still glazed over on her phone.

"Losers?" Carissa sat up. "They're freshmen! Of course they're losers! We were losers on our first day too."

"Speak for yourself," Sarah said coolly.

"Oh, come on, Sarah, when I first met you, you hardly ever said a word."

Sarah sat up and clicked off her phone. "Yeah, and the guys *loved* it."

"Those guys are gone now," Carissa said as she climbed out of bed. She was on the verge of crossing a line, and she knew it.

"Well, all of the guys in our grade are either dickheads or gross. When you're a freshman, you've got nowhere to go but up."

"That's not true," Carissa said, thankful for Sarah's casual tone. "What about Birdie?"

"Oh, Birdie's an ass." Sarah said this so emphatically it caught Carissa off guard. Was there something she didn't know?

"What do you mean? Birdie's not an ass."

"He likes the sound of his own voice. He's full of himself. A cocky ass."

Carissa blushed. "He's *confident*, not cocky."

"So you've got a crush on him, don't you?"

People often turned their heads when they saw Carissa and Sarah hanging out, even though their close friendship was no kept secret. It didn't bother Carissa as much as it presumably bothered Sarah. At St. Dominic's, someone's reputation preceded them. Everybody knew, or at least thought they knew, everything about everyone. And Carissa and Sarah just didn't add up. School sweetheart and school...punk-slut? School feisty-piece-of-ass? Wait, that was mean. Although Carissa always thought her butt was nicer than Sarah's...

*There I go again.*

It was moments like these, however, that made Carissa feel as though Sarah was the only person who knew her. There was no sense in being coy around Sarah, because God knows Sarah was going to say whatever was on her mind. She probably knew for months, maybe even years, that Carissa had a crush on Birdie, yet never brought it up. But why bring it up now?

"How'd you know?"

"Carissa, sweetie, honey, you are a lot of things. A lot of great things. But you aren't subtle."

So Sarah had been keeping an eye on Carissa. Sarah cared, in spite of all of her diatribes against crushes and mushy shit, against someone like Grace Martin and her lovey-dovey future hubby Mark, against anything more than just a casual hookup—Sarah actually *did* care! Or at least pretended to care enough for Carissa.

"You also left your little journal thingy out on your desk," Sarah then said. "The prompt: Do you have a crush on anybody? The answer, 09/10/16: *maybe, there's a cute boy in my history class.* The answer, 09/10/17: *Birdie.* The answer, today:—"

"Okay, I get it!" Carissa said, and so much for all that.

Sarah broke out into a fit of laughter and fell back onto the bed.

Carissa, at once embarrassed and annoyed, stood still in the center of the room with her hands tucked under her arms.

"You!" Sarah shot up again, cutting out of her laughter. "You never told me!" Her tone was disarmingly angry.

"You said you hated that stuff!"

"I *love* that stuff!"

Just then Jess barged in, clad in flannel pajamas and holding a family-sized bag of Smartfood.

"There's a bunch of freshman girls in my room right now eating junk food and sitting on the floor," she said through a mouthful of popcorn. "Care to join?"

Sarah stayed in the room to call her grandmother while Carissa and Jess walked down the hall to Jess' room. Carissa grabbed a handful of Smartfood and tried her best to eat it without spilling crumbs onto the floor. Last year her old dorm's sophomore floor had a big mice problem, and Carissa wasn't keen on the idea of reliving those terrifying rodent-laden shower excursions or hearing those late-night discomforting squeaks as she tried to fall asleep. She'd Googled time and time again *can mice climb up bedposts?*

Jess' room was much more decadently furnished than hers, with a blue kaleidoscopic tapestry and plush pillows and a fuzzy purple area rug and a lava lamp. It screamed 'dorm room' in all the ways Carissa found comforting and Sarah found nauseating. Four girls sat cross-legged on the floor, passing around a box of Wheat Thins. Carissa was determined to learn their names, to know their faces, know where they were from, who they liked, and who they disliked. She wanted to be the cool upperclassman.

Jess introduced Carissa to the girls, who went around and introduced themselves in turn. Adele ("Like the singer"), Jo ("J-O"), Cate ("with a 'C'"), and Avni. Adele and Jo were both from Virginia and were roommates. Cate and Avni were from Cambridge, MA, and Beijing, respectively. Carissa bonded with Cate first, as she too lived in Cambridge.

"Whereabouts do you live?" Carissa asked.

Carissa had never heard of the street Cate lived on, and vice versa. They weren't familiar with each other's favorite Cambridge coffee spots or pizza places, they got their hair cut at different salons, and seemed to have different geographical understandings of the layout of Harvard Square. Frustrated and suddenly unconfident in her own knowledge of her hometown, Carissa switched her focus to Avni. How did an Indian girl wind up living in Beijing?

"Wow, Beijing, that's so cool. How long have you lived there?" Carissa asked.

To make a long story short, Avni's family hopped around a lot. Raised in Chennai (which apparently was the fourth-largest city in India), then to Australia, a brief stint in San Francisco, then Tokyo, and now Beijing.

Carissa, still hooked on being the cool upperclassman, mentioned that she was quite worldly herself, having vacationed in Chile, South Africa, the Alps, and Costa Rica. "But I've never been to Asia," she added. "It's next on my list."

Jo and Adele, *no that one's Adele and that one's Jo*, went to the same private middle school in Virginia together and insisted on living together at St. Dom's.

"Besties," they said. Knowing St. Dom's, they'd probably stop talking to each other completely by the time they were Carissa's age.

The way the freshmen introduced and talked about themselves was all well-rehearsed. St. Dom's had a three-day orientation where the spry newcomers were subjected to obscene amounts of name-games, introductions, interrogations, and explanations. Carissa almost wanted to ask them what their favorite flavor of ice cream was, but she wasn't sure they'd understand that it was a joke before rattling off "cookie dough" and the like.

"We were talking about their classes and teachers before I went to grab you," Jess said. "Jo and Avni are both in Mr. L's math class."

"That guy's a total pushover," Carissa said. "If you want an A, just ask him for help after class every week or so. He'll practically do your homework for you, and he'll give you more partial credit on tests."

The freshmen girls looked ready to bust out pens and paper to take notes. It was funny, thinking back to her freshman math class, her freshman self. At the time, she was really grateful of how patient and helpful Mr. L was. For some reason, geometry just didn't come as easy to her as algebra. Pre-Calc this semester would probably kick her ass.

They all laughed about some faculty members, Jess and Carissa filling the newbies in on who to get to know and who to avoid. They talked about fall sports and if the freshmen really, actually had to, like, totally follow the lights-out rule at 10:30. They talked about the weather, which had been brutally hot. They talked about how tasty Wheat Thins were, the freshmen holding dear that a mutual appreciation of Wheat Thins could be the grounds for a real friendship. They talked about that morning's Chapel, Nick's, and what to do if they couldn't find their student-checker.

"So do either of you have boyfriends?" Adele asked. She was clearly the loudest, the proudest, the most sociable. Jo must have been living in her shadow for years.

As Jess explained how the boys were mostly gross, Carissa twirled her hair.

"Cate says that freshman girls mostly get with sophomore guys. Is that true?" Avni asked.

Cate shoved her and insisted she hadn't phrased it quite like that, not like that's not what she meant.

While Carissa and Jess looked at each other, unsure of how to answer the question, Sarah knocked on the door once before barging in.

"What's up freshmen," she said.

Carissa leaned back and tilted her head to look at Sarah. "Hey sis, help us out. Avni here wants to know if freshman girls are supposed to get with sophomore guys."

"A junior works in a pinch," Sarah said. "Best avoid seniors though. Shit gets messy."

Adele laughed, while Jo and Cate looked distraught. Avni pressed on: "But isn't that illegal?"

"Is ripping a Juul illegal?" Sarah shot back. "Don't worry about the law. Worry about the rules. And if you're going to break the rules, don't get caught."

Carissa's understanding of herself as the cool upperclassman took on a new meaning then. She wasn't the cool role model upperclassman, the example to follow. She was the cool upperclassman because she roomed with the badass Sarah Donner, who didn't give a damn what people thought of her and who broke the rules and who hated Wheat Thins.

///Meanwhile, in the boys dorm, Todd and Birdie were debating who the hottest three girls in their grade were, now accounting for summer developments. Mark was in the room as well, working on history homework. As soon as Mark left to take a piss, Birdie and Todd turned to each other and said, in unison, "Grace is totally in the top three now." Later, after having to agree to disagree on who the hottest girl in the grade was, Birdie pondered whether or not he'd ever stop being such an objectifying douche. Todd, to alleviate Birdie's existential conundrum while maintaining a sense of dignity, blamed their recent conversation not on any personal shortcomings in respect or decency, but rather on the oversaturation of beautiful women on social media combined with the esoteric degeneracy of living in an all-boys dormitory from such a young age. Birdie, content to agree to likewise retain his own dignity, knew it was bullshit. Todd did as well.///

# THE FIRST FRIDAY OF
# SUMMER. 11:28 PM.

—

"Okay, Todd, listen *very* carefully." Birdie said as though he were talking to a young child or his dog Fido. He was slumped on the couch, legs up on the coffee table. Carissa huddled next to him on her phone. He tapped his Juul to prove it was indeed flashing red: out of battery. "You're going to go to the main house, and you're going to very quietly make your way upstairs. You know where my room is. In my underwear drawer there should be a new pack of mint pods, and the charger should be plugged in behind my bed. You get all of that?"

Todd was leaning over the back of the couch. "Bed. Underwear. Yep."

"Good boy," Birdie said and patted Todd's messy brown hair. "Just don't wake up my parents, and we'll be all set."

"I'll be back 'fore you know it." Todd said, and he rolled off the couch to set off on his quest.

Everyone had disappeared, really. Birdie thought he had heard Chris say that a couple of them were going to go out to the beach to smoke. Jess had put Sarah to bed. Mark and Grace were somewhere, probably, having one of those drunk conversations where it's revealed that everything was all just a big misunderstanding. And if it weren't for Carissa, Birdie probably would have tried to stop their little chat from happening in the first place. For Mark's sake. He'd been having these weird little episodes, slips into the void, and Birdie thought the whole mess was Grace's fault in the first place. They definitely weren't bad shrooms they'd taken; just bad timing.

Carissa looked back to see if Todd was really gone (he'd taken the 'be quiet' order to such an extreme as to slip out of the guest house without making a sound). In doing so, turning her head, she readjusted her body such that when she turned back around, she'd naturally be leaning on Birdie's shoulder.

"How long do you think it'll take Todd?" she asked.

Birdie put his arm around her. "It should only take him less than five minutes," he said. "So it'll probably take him ten."

And in those ten minutes, what exactly would happen here? A bit of cuddling, some glances. Carissa was still on her phone, swiping through Instagram stories. What was Birdie's move?

It was probably more like eight minutes now, and counting. If they were still like this when Todd came back, what was the move? And how long ago did Chris say they were going to the beach? When would they be back?

Carissa yawned. She tried her best to conceal it, but Birdie felt it. He yawned back, trying his best to hide it as well. "A call and response raging against the dying of the light," as McMahon would say.

She threw her phone onto the table. Seven minutes. And that was all assuming Todd was really as drunk as Birdie thought he was.

He was rock hard, hardly trying to hide it.

Here's what he should've done, it came to him now. He should've told Todd that he and Carissa would go to his bedroom to get the stuff for the Juul, that Todd was too drunk and he'd make a racket. That way Birdie would be alone, in his bedroom, with Carissa. And they'd have the Juul.

That should've been Plan A. Because there wasn't a Plan B. This was Plan B: sitting here, twiddling thumbs, waiting for someone to come break the tension, kill their precious privacy.

"Do you think Todd's getting there alright?" Carissa asked. She looked up at Birdie, who turned his head to meet her gaze.

He could kiss her now, but then what? Where would they go?

"I have an idea," Birdie said, purposely enunciating his words to push his lips closer to Carissa's. "If you *want*, *we* can climb up to the *roof*, that *way we'll* be able to see if Todd turns on my bed*room* lights." He licked his lips. "Or, *more* likely, *we'll* be able to see if Todd's passed out in the yard."

It certainly wasn't his most inspired idea, but it would solve the privacy problem. And sure, maybe they wouldn't get very far on the roof. The steep incline would prohibit safely performing most sexual activity. But a romantic make-out under the stars, that'd be fine. He probably was too drunk to really gain much from anything beyond that anyway.

"Let's go, quickly, before we miss him!" Carissa exclaimed, jumping up off the couch. Birdie figured he'd guide her up by her hand, but she seemed eager to trail blaze.

They went up the stairs, Carissa shushing him as they passed Sarah's room. They went through the bathroom window and crawled out onto the roof. They had to scale the top of the guest house then climb to the other side for a view of the main house.

"I don't see any lights on," Carissa commented after they gained solid footing. "Which is your bedroom?"

"It's the one on the right, there, right there," he said, leaning over and pointing, brushing his arm over Carissa's shoulder. They were speaking in hushed tones, not (as Birdie imagined) to avoid waking up his parents, but to avoid signaling to any nearby friends that they were up there.

A light went on in the main house, though not the one Birdie had pointed out. It was the bedroom to the left of his, Maud's bedroom. They watched in silence as, shortly thereafter, Maud's light went out again. Then Birdie's room lit up.

"He made it," Carissa said, and gesturing with her fists *Hooray* she turned to face Birdie.

And then, right then, Carissa and her lips mere inches away, and with everything twinkling in the starlight, eight thoughts raced through Birdie's mind, more or less in this order:

Carissa was absolutely stunningly gorgeous; but her breath was quite bad, assuming that was her breath he was smelling; he was far more drunk than he initially wagered, and resting on that roof was actually a good bit of work; this might be a thought, or it might be a memory, but Carissa *definitely* wanted this more than he did; but hell, he wanted this too; then something about Henry Dinelli, of all people; Maury killed somebody; and finally, her boobs weren't as big as he'd thought they were.

So he didn't lean in. Instead, he turned houseward, watching what he could make out of Todd's silhouette pacing around his room. But maybe his eyes were just buzzing off the booze.

Obviously Carissa didn't say, "Oh," like that, like *oh, well,* but the sentiment translated through the crickets and the wind. So there they sat, silent, both watching the light from Birdie's window. Although occasionally maybe Carissa would sneak a glance at Birdie who, needless to say was halfway flaccid, doing his best not to show how suddenly difficult it was to stay still on the slanted roof.

And then the light turned off, and it was darker.

Where words typically came naturally spouting from Birdie's mouth, here there were none. It was a guilt, of sorts. It was all happening again. The spurn. The unsaid and unintended *no* which accomplished more slight than any formal declination. Birdie picked at a scab on his thumb and hoped Carissa would say—

"I feel silly," she said, and for once in Birdie's life had his thoughts translated to others' actions in real-time.

But now he was on the defensive, defending either his own dignity or hers, he couldn't quite tell. "No," he managed, feeble and cracked. "No, it's…Don't feel silly."

And you know, he thought she'd be crying. But Carissa didn't cry.

Birdie more than anything wanted to be with Mark, somewhere else, doing nothing.

"No, you don't have to feel bad," she said. She swatted a mosquito from her thigh. "I get it, like, seriously, don't worry."

Birdie remembered the seventh thought that had run through his head in that moment of ill-fated pseudo-clarity and felt the weight of his body against the house, actively resisting the urge to sink and slide downwards, off the edge. It wasn't her fault, none of it.

"Give me a minute," he said. "I have something to tell you. It's just the words haven't formed yet."

Was that too misleading? Was that too *forthcoming-pro-fession-of-love-and-I-want-this-I-really-really-do-but-just-not-when-I'm-drunk-not-like-this*? Admittedly, only such a thought could pass through Birdie's head. Only such a circumstance, such a thwarted climax. He always thought of himself as the main character of his story, not realizing that everyone else did the same. Because to Birdie that would be an impossibility. No one else could be the main character of their own story because no other story existed except Birdie's.

So what was he going to say? He'd bought himself some time. What was his move? And why the fuck did he always *need* a move in the first place? Something, perhaps everything, from his mandatory mindfulness seminar freshmen year had completely gone unacknowledged. It was never *now*, it was always *what's next*.

And truth be told, Birdie never really had his way with chicks. With *girls*. Not that he didn't like them, or fantasize about them, or that he was, like, *gay*, or anything. He just had a hard time letting himself hook up with somebody. Maybe it was a not-like-this ordeal every time he got close, only that was bullshit because if not then, now, then when? Was that what was happening now, a stubborn psychosomatic refusal of circumstance? Of less-than-perfection?

Was it *really* the breath?

Was it really *Maury*?

Carissa was being awfully patient while Birdie pondered what to say, perhaps tragically patient. But then it came to him, not the thesis of his statement but at least the introduction, the angle in, the hook.

"I want you to let me finish," he said, eyes keen on the side door of the main house awaiting Todd, "because I know it's gonna sound bad at first."

He cleared his throat.

"Okay, Carissa, *darling*, you are the bee's knees, the cat's meow, every damn flattering idiom. I could profess. But here's the thing, and this is really only part of the thing, now that I say it," and he turned to face her, "Carissa, it's not you. It's Maury."

And she sighed angrily, as expected.

"But hear me out, hear me out! It's been Maury since long before his, uh, well it's been Maury since long before he fucking killed someone. Like, when we were gonna go on a date back in January, and I had to cancel, even though I cancelled for reasons which had absolutely nothing to do with Maury, or you for that matter…Before I cancelled, I was nervous. I was intimidated. And this was all pre-*fucking*-murder, you know? Obviously you know. And it's definitely not what I imagine you want to hear, but really Maury was like a big brother to me, and you were like his little sister…"

Todd stumbled out of the backdoor and kind of zig-zagged toward the back of the guest house until he was out of sight. They both watched in silence.

"Okay, let me explain, really, cause I've been doing a shit job. And I talk a lot. I extend simple things out to their baser elements until there's nothing left to talk about because you're not even sure where I began…Alright. Simply put, I think you are incredibly attractive, and obviously I wanted to hook up with you just now. That's why we're sitting here on the roof. I just can't. And it's certainly not you, and even though I've brought Maury into all this, I really think it's mostly me, and a little bit of him. I don't know. I can't. I've only kissed one girl before. Not that that's important, or relevant. Like, *fuck*. Carissa I want to be friends with you, and I want this new little friend group we've got somehow someway here with us tonight to be, like, a *thing* throughout senior year, and you don't really wanna get with me, trust me, I'm not boyfriend material, I'm an ass, really, truly, just ask any of the guys, or even Grace. I'm sure she's told you. Can we just not hook up? Sorry."

As he finished he realized that there was no way to respond to all of what he'd said other than emotionally, instantaneously, recklessly. So he prepared for an onslaught, a diatribe, a something. He prepared to take back some of what he'd said, to rephrase the rest. Instead—unfortunately, unpredictably, unbearably—Carissa said nothing.

At least for a while. Eventually she said, "Okay, I get it," and then, "could you just leave me alone for a while?"

To which Birdie said "Yes, of course," without realizing that meant he should leave the rooftop, like, pronto.

So Carissa added, "Like, now? I wanna be alone out here."

As Birdie crawled back over the top of the house to the bathroom window and, as he crawled ungracefully through, clanging and banging against the faucet and towel rack, somehow more drunk than he was on the way out, the only thing he could think about was *where is Todd with my Juul charger?*

///*As it turned out, Todd was on the couch downstairs, shirtless, sipping whiskey from a wineglass. The Juul charger was plugged into the wall beside him. Birdie plopped the Juul onto the charger and sat next to Todd in silence, taking a swig from the whiskey wineglass without asking where either had come from.*///

# WEDNESDAY, JULY 31ST, 2019. 5:05 PM.

---

The weather was crap, all cloudy and cold. It had rained spasmodically throughout the day, yet the sun always remained obscured behind the thin gray overcast. Only sixty-four degrees in late July, and Frank was supposed to believe climate change was, like, a real thing?

For the first time in his entire life Frank had started to wear jeans, which before he always thought were kind of faggy, but they ended up being super comfortable once he found the right pair. He was turning eighteen soon, and his Mom told him he couldn't go through life wearing only St. D's sweatpants in the winter and khaki shorts in the summer.

He had on a gray crew-neck St. D's sweatshirt, that was actually his father's from back when his father went there. Frank's Dad was a freshman when Birdie's Dad was a senior, back in the eighties. They didn't remember each other, though. Frank thought it was cool to rock the old sweatshirt, with its faded red lettering and little holes in the armpits. It was a man's sweatshirt, fully lived in. Just not by him.

He'd decided to go into the woods to make the phone call. There were these, like, trails, Frank didn't know what else to call them, in the woods behind his house. Even though they were trail-like, they were wide enough for a car to pass through. Frank didn't like to call them trails because his friends who went hiking and wore Patagonia and shit once scoffed at him for bringing them to these 'trails.' Anyway, the kind-of-trails led up to a massive, defunct Nashua water tank. The concrete structure was now riddled with various graffiti'd calling cards and name decals

He called Birdie after slipping his AirPods into his ears.

Birdie answered with, "Frankie, you'll never believe this."

"Can you hear me alright?" Frank asked.

"Yes, never mind that, so long as you can hear me alright. Listen to this Frankie, I just fucking *cut my dick*. It's fucking *bleeding*, Frankie. Bleeding. My dick."

"How'd you cut your dick?"

"It was a little prick, that's all."

"Is that what you call it?" Frank was impressed he could quip on the fly.

"No, but it might be what I start calling you." Birdie laughed through the pain. Never mind that, Frankie. My dick, it's bleeding."

"Should I call you back?"

"No, I'll put you on speaker. What's up? Fuck!"

Frank wasn't exactly sure how to angle-in on this one. "Just calling to see what's up, is all," he said.

"I told you what's up. Talk to me man. What's good with you? I'm going to mute myself so you can't hear the inevitable agonized wails when I try to throw some, like, fucking disinfectant or something on the *gash*, but I'll be listening. If you run out of things to say, just start listing your favorite things about me."

"Birdie, you shouldn't—," but he could tell Birdie had already muted himself. The low-grade static had cut out to sheer silence.

Around Frank were white trees, mostly birches with bark peeling off like paper, though there were some scattered quaking aspens as well. He could tell a quaking aspen from a birch by the dark eyes on aspens where branches once were. It was creepy stuff to see those eyes all looking at him, with occasional thick droplets falling on or near him from the canopy above in this gray, heavy air.

"Tell you what, Birdo, I'm walking through the woods right now, and there are all these, like, *eyes* in the trees. You know how when you get high and sometimes get that feeling that something's watching you? It's like that. Except I guess I am kinda high, so it's like, *exactly* like that."

He imagined Birdie's wincing on the other end of the line. How does someone manage to cut their dick?

"Anyway," Frank continued, unsure if Birdie was listening. "I was, uh, calling to tell you something. I just thought it's something you'd, like, wanna know. Maybe you won't care, but like, if you were gonna hear it from someone it's probably best it be me."

Birdie unmuted himself. "FUCK I tell ya man this was *definitely* a bad idea. God damnit! And what, are you about to tell me that Henry killed himself or something?"

The line went silent again, muted. "No, no no no. Jesus man, not that. Although I guess someone should reach out to him. That's not the point. Look, I'm just gonna say it." He cracked his knuckles and looked around at all the eyes staring at him, judging him. Primordial judgment, ancient shit. "Alright man, look, like, I *kind of* hooked up with Carissa that night at your house like a month and a half ago."

He was met with more silence. Should he keep going? Was Birdie in shock? Well, Birdie was definitely in shock and a lot of pain, but was Birdie, like, really taken aback? In a bad way?

Just as Frank was about to elaborate on the details, Birdie chimed back in: "Sorry, chief, I was over on the other side of the room. You hooked up with Carissa?"

"Yeah."

"When?"

"I told you, at your little party thing."

"I know, but like, *when*?"

"Are you mad?"

"No I'm not mad. Well, I'm mad, yes, not at you. I'm mad at myself."

"What? How is this your fault?"

"About my dick, Frankie! My dick!"

"Oh. So you're really not mad?"

"Not at all, man. Good for you. She's a dream. She's so fucking hot. Wait, does Sarah know?"

"No."

"When exactly did you hook up with Carissa?"

"I dunno, like after Chris and Jess and I got back from smoking."

"Where?"

"Like, upstairs man."

"Where?"

"Dude, in the bathroom."

"How?"

"I dunno. I went up to like check on Sarah, and Carissa was crawling in through the bathroom window right as I was taking a piss. She just kind of grabbed me and kissed me."

"Did she say anything?"

"Well, yeah, she said she wanted to hook up, unless I had any, like, objections."

"Really? That's all she said?" Birdie's voice cracked.

"And to not tell anybody."

"So why are you telling me?"

"I dunno man, I thought you maybe had a crush on her or something."

"A crush? No way, José. Who else knows?"

"Nobody, unless Carissa's told somebody, but, like, I doubt she has."

"I thought you were with Sarah," Birdie said, his tone now confrontational.

"No, we were never, like, an official thing or anything. Besides, we haven't hooked up in ages."

"You guys hooked up at the end of the school year."

"But, like, that was ages ago."

"It was *like* ten days before you hooked up with Carissa."

"Are you sure you aren't mad?"

"Why didn't you just hook up with Sarah? You were going to check on her, right?"

"She was sleeping."

"So you just decided you'd hook up with Carissa then?"

"No, like I told you, she just kinda materialized in the bath-room and initiated the whole thing." Frank was impressed he'd thought of the word *materialized* so naturally.

"Carissa was drunk that night, Frank. She was drunk. I mean, why would she want to hook up with you?"

"Are you sure you're not mad?"

A cyclist whizzed by, nearly grazing Frank's left side. Frank spun around, dazed. One of his AirPods fell out of his ear somewhere under a pile of forest detritus. As he bent down to look for it, the other fell out. Birdie had been saying something like "I just think it's—." He finally found both the AirPods, which were actually, like, really a bitch to find sometimes, and lodged them back into his ears.

"Hello? Birdie?"

He checked his phone. The call had been disconnected; Frank had no service. The graffiti'd landmark was up ahead.

Frank made his way to the back of the concrete tank and was saddened to see someone had partially scribbled over the spot where he, Chris, Ty, Benzi, and Rico had painted their autographs three years earlier. It was one of those things, right after eighth grade graduation (because Catholic middle schools have like *actual* graduations), they'd all come out here at night with flashlights and spray paint and marked the tank, immortalizing themselves. Someone had painted over the "i" in "Benzi" to spell out "Benzene gives you cancer." What the fuck was Benzene?

Frank often missed those guys, especially when he got high with his new friends. His St. D's friends. His 'boarding school' friends. Benzi, Ty, and those guys all went to Nashua High School North, public and big. They all hung out after school together and got high together and made new friends and had all these new stories and met all these hot chicks. Frank, in the meantime, was away in a dorm room jacking off, studying, getting high with Birdie and Todd, and occasionally hooking up with Sarah fucking Donner.

Frank never really considered himself homesick, even though most guys were homesick even when they claimed they weren't. Frank, if anything, was friendsick. Sick of his new friends, sick for his old ones.

*///When Frank got back home, he had an unread text from Birdie:* I think Mark and Grace also hooked up that night FYI. I'm like 90% sure. Bad night for the boys all around.///

# SATURDAY, MAY 25TH, 2019. 9:00 PM.

———

Sarah knew it wasn't the best idea to have pregamed Spring Fling with Todd and Frank. Hell, even Birdie thought it was a bad idea. Last year they'd busted a couple of seniors for being drunk at the Fling. Now there were all sorts of e-mails and PSA's about being smart and safe at the last dance of the year. *Don't Get Sprung and Flung Outta School!* or *Finish Strong! You're Diploma Depends On It!* or *Let's Make 2019 The Year Where No Seniors Get Expelled!* and the like. And yes, at least three different faculty members of varying authority had green-lit "*You're Diploma Depends On It!*" to be printed en masse. The seniors were graduating in thirty-six hours, so maybe faculty roamers and chaperones would only be paying attention to them. And it's not like they'd all got hammered, or anything. Sarah was dancing with Carissa and Grace and Em and Jess, and none of them had wanted to drink (none of them would have been offered some anyway) but Sarah was safe. She was drunk, but also huddled in a circle of sobriety, of laughs, of dance, of cheering when a good song came on.

It made her want to puke. In fact, it *really* made her want to puke. Where was Frank? Of course he was over by the water cooler, chatting with Todd. They didn't look drunk at all.

"Where are you going, sis?" Carissa tugged on her summer dress.

"Oh, I'm fine," she managed to say before spinning around to go get Frank.

Sarah navigated the clusters of freshmen dancing, the sophomores slumping, the juniors all looking around, and the few seniors who actually dared to show face looking all sentimental and happy. She made it to the cooler, grabbed Frank's cup of water from his hand, and chugged it, ice cold.

"Frank let's go," she said and took his hand.

Todd said something. Frank hollered back, but she was already leading him away.

The walk to their spot—a bit of prime real estate by the old soccer nets Frank had inherited from Mark after Grace had given him the shaft—involved circumambulating around various street lights and dorm-awning lights and hightailing it out of the way of the vectors of roamer's flashlights to avoid being spotted by bloodthirsty faculty. Of course, Sarah and Frank also had to avoid, altogether in a roundabout sort of way, the newly installed industrial field-lights, dubbed the "Fuck-You Lights" by of course Birdie. These lights, rather than deterring students from hooking up, actually forced them to hook up in near bacchanalian proximity. Committed to their furtive strut, and still spinning physically and mentally from the alcohol, neither Sarah nor Frank said much until they got to their soccer net.

Frank collapsed onto the ground, sighing in what was either relief or discomfort. He slouched against the goal post, facing the collapsed net, and unzipped his blue shorts.

Over near the stand of trees separating the fields from the road, not too far off from where Sarah stood, was the freshman Adele. Her chrome tube top shimmered in the dark, reflecting the Fuck-You light. Though her vision was starting to swirl, not to mention blur, Sarah could swear Adele was *only* wearing that tube top.

Frank was moaning a bit, perhaps snoring. Sarah rested on the post and pulled out her phone, unable to really remember how to do any of the things she'd normally do when she pulled out her phone. So she just stared at the buzzing home screen, a picture of her and Carissa and Jess from last year sitting on The Lawn. A notification from some freshman boy requesting to follow her on Instagram obscured the three girls' faces.

It was entirely possible that IG user @timthompson was the horned-up, supine boy currently being straddled by Adele, come to think of it. *Supine* was on yesterday's weekly vocabulary quiz. Sarah could no longer discern Adele's top. Yes, she remembered, because Adele thought maybe he was related to Frank Thomson. Frank's last name didn't have a 'p' in it, though, a distinction which didn't explain to Adele why the guy she was hooking up with always mentioned Sarah Donner.

Frank just kind of sat there, unzipped, motionless, and not inviting Sarah to come to him. His shorts were most likely unzipped platonically, to give his growing gut some breathing room.

Sometimes things just flush like a wave, very suddenly, and you realize you've only got like ten seconds max to get to somewhere you won't make a belching mess of yourself, at least not in an inconvenient location. Unfortunately for Sarah, in an open field cluttered with licentious teenagers (also a vocab word), there was no convenient location. Sarah traded one goal post for another and lurched forward, falling to her knees, and rested her left shoulder on the post, pulled her hair back, and puked onto the grass, all brown and red and liquidy.

And then the spitting, the gasping, the nose-purging, the threat of a second wave which manifested into a harmless burp, the wiping of the nose, the heavy breathing came with Frank behind her asking "What's going on?" Then the flare-up of tears overpowered her.

By the time Sarah had collected herself, as far as anyone who'd just thrown up in a soccer net could, the stench's ripple throughout the field had reached Adele and Tim Thompson, who were loudly complaining, as well as one or two other couples nearer to campus, similarly whining.

Needless to say, Sarah had to get out of there like *pronto*, although nothing about her current state really allowed her to do anything *pronto*. She kind of groaned in Frank's direction, both of them slumped against opposite goal posts. Frank gave her a thumbs up, like *all good?* And, well, that was really just the funniest thing. Not ha-ha funny the way people often discern laughter as not being ha-ha funny, but more like absolutely humiliatingly, deflatingly funny. Whatever the opposite of 'we'll look back on this and laugh' was, when you're in a situation which seems irredeemably shitty. Only now Sarah laughed, knowing full fucking well she would soon look back on this and cry.

Luckily Chris and Jess had been one of the shaded whining couples gone flaccid from the stink and passed by the soccer net on their way back to campus. Jess helped Sarah back into their dorm, which was apparently a whole fucking operation (not-getting-caught-wise). Jess put her in the shower, which was at first way too cold then way too hot, but by then Jess had left and so Sarah had to reach up herself to turn the knob to change the temperature but her ass kind of slipped on the shower floor (because she was sitting) and just, like, completely gave out so she banged her elbow real hard on the ground, luckily not her funny bone though, which either way kind of snapped her awake, and the scalding water was just like letting her *have it* right at her face, making it hard to breathe, but she then got up and was able to be up and rest against the wall of the shower and the water wasn't actually *that* hot—it just took some getting used to.

Jess came in to check on her maybe fifteen minutes later, but by then Sarah was drying off.

It wasn't 10:30 yet, obviously, because Carissa wasn't back and she could hear the faint sounds of pop music from the dance. Jess had laid out some of Sarah's pajamas on the bed and put a mug of water on her desk.

"Chris says he took care of Frank all right," Jess said as Sarah, naked aside from her pajama shorts she'd ungracefully slipped on under her towel, hopped into bed.

Sarah didn't respond, or at least she intended to say something but couldn't really think of anything to say until it got to the point where she just decided not to respond. She liked laying there, half-naked, with someone in the room. Even if it was Jess. She felt comfortable, a similar comfort she felt laying naked next to Frank. Only Jess was standing far away by the door.

Her body buzzed pleasantly. She asked Jess if she'd tuck her in, which Jess did, although it was clear that Jess' parents never really tucked her in when she was little. As Jess brought up the comforter over Sarah's chest, Sarah thought about leaning in to kiss her. She didn't, though.

"Lights on or lights off?" Jess asked, making her way back to the door.

Sarah wanted the lights on because she didn't want to fall asleep yet. She wanted to wait until Carissa came back, because she wanted to talk with Carissa. Not about anything in particular, really. She just, like, wanted to talk. So Jess left the lights on and slipped out the door.

Some time passed. She thought of Frank, and their pseudo-relationship, although she couldn't really formulate much in the way of coherent thinking. All of her thoughts manifested into actual strung-out sentences, her having to actually enunciate each word of every thought in her head in order to focus on it. She thought of the memorized vocabulary words. She didn't really think much of how she'd been ready just then to kiss Jess, because like that was just a totally normal thought right? She thought of Chris and of something she'd said to him way back when that was honestly kind of racist and made her hate herself. The pulsing music stopped, seemingly mid-song, outside. She waited for Carissa to come back and thought of the pile of vomit she'd left on the field, until she realized it was easier to think with her eyes closed. Then the thoughts all blended together in a swirl of unenunciation until she drifted off into that place you drift off to when you fall asleep without trying.

She awoke, who knows how long afterward, and Carissa was seated in a towel staring at her desk with her head in her hands. She must have been on the phone with someone, because she was saying, "...it was a pretty stupid thought, anyway."

Only there was no phone. Sarah rolled onto her side and discovered she was wearing a shirt.

"Oh, you're up," Carissa said without much care. "We put a shirt on you. Your boobs were just kind of out."

In spite of anything in the way of intention, Sarah didn't respond.

"Can I talk you through something?" Carissa asked. "Or more like talk myself through something out loud?"

Again, nothing more than like a half-nod, sideways of course.

"I was like just randomly thinking this today. I don't really know why, just one of those thoughts you get sometimes. It's a would-you-rather sort of thing. One option is that every night before you go to bed, you flip a coin. If it's heads, the next day will be the best day of your life. If it's tails, the next day will be the worst day in your life. But so the first option is that you flip the coin."

Carissa materialized a coin seemingly from thin air. "Or, okay, the next option is that you don't flip the coin. That there is no coin. The condition being that tomorrow won't be the best or worst day of your life. Always. Does that make sense?"

Again, another sideways nod. Sarah had a hard time really knowing when Carissa was depressed with a capital 'D.' Like should Sarah treat everything Carissa said as though it really meant something else? Was everything getting at something else, like, some deeper meaning? But then if she always treated Carissa that way, always hung onto whatever she said, wouldn't Carissa feel like spoken-down to and then only get sadder? Or was it more sad? 'Crestfallen' was another vocab word, even if it was pretty sound-it-out-and-you-can-kinda-tell-what-it-means. Or maybe Sarah just thought that Carissa would feel bad because she, Sarah, didn't want to put in the effort to always care, and it was like a self-defensive sort of justification disguised as empathy?

These thoughts made Sarah's head spin on a good night. This was not a good night.

"It's linear, one way. If you decide you're going to flip the coin each night, then your days will keep getting better and better. Some days will be unimaginable ecstasy eventually, but conversely, those other days will keep getting darker and lower-…er, you know?" Carissa said. She flipped the coin in her hand, and closed her fist before looking at it. "Or you just accept that your best and worst days are already behind you. Then what are you living for, going forward?"

"I don't like either," Sarah mustered the wherewithal to say. She pronounced it *eee-ther.*

"I don't like either, either," Carissa responded, *eee-ther,* then *aye-ther.*

"Is it eee-ther or aye-ther?" Sarah asked, smiling in a manner which made her drool, but who cared.

"I don't think it's either," Carissa responded, only she wasn't smiling.

"You mean neither."

"I don't think it matters which."

She tossed the coin onto Sarah's bed without looking to see which side it had landed on. Sarah took that as a cue that maybe this was totally just something Carissa needed to figure out on her own, it being such a painfully trite symbol of something Sarah couldn't quite put her finger on.

///*"Frank, like, Jesus fucking shit. Look at me. Look at me. It's Chris. Look at me. Hey! Buddy! All right, we're about to walk into the dorm. You are fucked up. This is what we're* gonna—Oh, for fuck sakes, zip up your shorts. Alright. Listen. We're gonna go in. Connolly's on duty. I need you to stand up straight. All you have to do is sign your name. And maybe answer one of those bullshit like 'evening boys' non-question questions. Can you do that? Is that a nod? I'm gonna slap you. Okay? Did that hurt? Sorry. I need you to do this. Piece of cake. You've got this."///

# THE SNOW DAY.
# 2:20 PM.

———

So, the pink elephants were *definitely* the weirdest part. It was all five minutes eyes opened, five minutes eyes shut, etc., etc. He opened or closed his eyes when it all became too much. When his eyes were open, things would eventually start to swirl and become far away, and each object had consequence and frightening potential. So then he'd shut his eyes. And sometimes, when his eyes were closed, he could still see. As if his eyes were still open. Or else it was the pink elephants.

Dozens of little cartoon pink elephants, *dancing*. Like can-can style, on some bastardized eight-bit vintage Donkey Kong arcade set of purple beams. Zooming in, zooming out. Dancing. Maybe they were wearing top-hats, or maybe their big old flappy ears were just bent awkwardly over their heads. But the elephants were definitely dancing.

And despite being absolutely outside (and absolutely within) himself, Mark was able to notice how fucking cliched it was, the whole Grateful Deadesque stock footage psychedelic imagery.

The word *shroooooooooms* looped and echoed and banged against the walls of his brain.

Then he'd open his eyes, ad hoc.

Right when shit hit the fan, about 300 years ago, he told Birdie to play that chill indie folk shit as a last-ditch effort to calm the fuck down. It was definitely better than the trap Frank had been blasting, and Mark tapped now his toes to the fingerpicked chords.

Oh, but fuck.

He thought he heard Frank say he was—

*Fuck me, that book is twisting.*

He closed his eyes.

He thought he heard Frank say he was going to get Birdie to get Henry to give to Frank, through Birdie, something for Mark.

*Frank, Birdie, Henry, Mark...*

Not the elephants this time, no. A boot. A *big* boot. That feeling when you realize before you fall asleep that you're about to fall asleep and pull yourself out of that unconscious stream-of-consciousness where the thoughts formulate independently—only Mark was stuck there. Witnessing his own unconsciousness, without the adrenaline to wake himself up.

A big boot, like, *big*. The size of a house, big. Brown leather. No foot, no leg, no body. Just a boot, walking on its own. Walking slowly, in the backyard. It's nighttime but it's light. And Mark's putting tiny stickers on blades of grass. The boot steps toward him, still a safe distance away. But the reverberations in the ground knock the stickers off of the grass. Maybe Grace is the boot. Oh, and the grass is wet, so it wasn't keeping the stickers well in the first place.

"Mark?"

So he opened his eyes. Yeah, fuck that big ass boot. Fuck that. *Fuck me.*

Did he respond? It felt like his lips had just moved, and his throat was tighter, but he couldn't remember saying anything.

"Okay," from Frank.

All this time, and Mark hadn't even wondered how Birdie's trip was going.

"Mark, take this." Speaking of Birdie.

And there he was, standing right in front of him. Mark was curled up in the fetal position on Birdie's bed.

"Please, don't touch me," Mark managed over the course of two minutes.

"You can swallow it or let it dissolve under your tongue," Birdie said.

He closed his eyes again, suppressing the urge to vomit.

"If you let it dissolve under your tongue, it will be super bitter and unpleasant, but it will kick in faster."

Next thing Mark knew, the bottom of his mouth had a hole in it. He tried to scream, but it came out as a whimper.

*Shroooooooms.*

"Aight, fuck, Mark, man, like, Okay I got this, here, spit it out," Frank held his hand by Mark's mouth.

What the fuck did he want him to spit out? Something burned under his tongue... burning. He slowly fished it out of his mouth with his fingers and placed the semi-dissolved pill in Frank's hand. A droopy line of spit tied Frank's hand to Mark's mouth.

"Fucking *gross.*"

Gross. It was gross, the body. Fuck, he was sitting up now. How long had he been sitting up? Had he ever really been lying down?

And now he was down again, eyes closed. He couldn't get the thought of the Cincinnati Bengals out of his head.

*What the fuck?*

Eyes open. Eyes closed. His ankles crossed. Suddenly, from his feet and shooting up his body. He was falling, like not really falling but like when you're about to fall asleep and then you fall off a cliff and you jolt up.

"Mark!" Birdie exclaimed. Or maybe it was Frank. His eyes were still closed.

He opened them to see Birdie's face, slightly twisted and twisting. Mark was sitting upright in Birdie's bed.

"Dude, you just yelled and shot up. Scared the shit out of me."

"How long was I asleep for?" Mark asked.

"You weren't asleep, dude."

"I just woke up, though."

What was happening? What time was it? It was dark outside.

"Dude, it's good to have you back," Birdie said. He patted him on the shoulder, lightly.

Frank walked into the room, wiping his hands on his pants.

"Frank, Mark woke up."

"But he wasn't sleeping?" Frank said, a statement as a question.

"No, he wasn't. I guess the Valium just kicked in."

"What time is it?" Mark asked. His hands were weak. He tried making a fist, but couldn't really squeeze.

"It's almost 7:30," Frank said. "Good thing you snapped out of it. Birdie and I had a whole fucking contingency plan for when Mr. Reeves came around for check-in, but it probably wasn't gonna work."

"I feel like shit," Mark said.

"You look like shit," Birdie and Frank said together. Birdie offered him water.

"I've gotta shit," Mark said. And it was coming on fast, too, now that he thought about it.

*///Frank and Birdie's plan (which probably wasn't gonna work) to convince a concerned Mr. Reeves that Mark was all right but couldn't talk right now, nor should he be brought to the Health Center: Step one: forcibly move Mark to the top bunk and tuck him deeply underneath the covers. Step two: get the freshman Miles to come down. Step three: Tuck Miles into Birdie's bed, hair out, face away from the door. Mark and Miles have similar hair. Step four: When Mr. Reeves walks in, put up a 'shhhhh' sign. Birdie was coming down from his own trip and was still acting a bit foolish, so Frank would do most of the talking. If Mr. Reeves insisted on seeing Mark's face, Frank and Birdie would both act surprised to see it was Miles sleeping in Birdie's bed all along. Miles, under no circumstance, was to snitch. He'd just come down to Birdie's room to play*

*Fortnite and fell asleep waiting for his turn. Frank and Birdie would then act concerned. Where's Mark? they'd ask. And this concern, this question, was not a lie. They did not know where Mark was at the moment. Well, they knew Mark was under the blankets on the top bunk. But they had no idea where that poor kid was.///*

# TUESDAY, DECEMBER 14TH, 2018. 6:12 PM.

—

It was after dinner, not that Carissa really ate much at dinner anyway. They were all in Carissa's room. Carissa and Sarah's room. *Sarah* and Carissa's room, maybe. Typical scene. Sarah was—and this was a first—studying for exams a week in advance. She had her AirPods in and was reading her history textbook at her desk. Grace sat next to Carissa, both of them on Carissa's bed. They were watching some YouTube video explaining what happened during the War of 1812, with cute little animated graphics.

"It's like, 1812 now, if you think about it," Jess said from the floor. She wasn't watching the video, per se, but she was learning through the audio. She then explained how it was December 2018, which like didn't *really* work, but, like, still. Carissa thought about mentioning that it was 18:12 military time, but didn't.

It was a pretty glum scene. Jess, Grace, and Carissa were all in APUSH together, a fun little acronym for AP U.S. History. Sarah was in plain old, regular U.S. History, but wasn't doing what one might consider hot in the class and totally needed to do pretty good on the final exam. Or so she told Carissa. And that info was for Carissa's ears only, because Carissa knew Sarah wouldn't want Grace to think she was dumb.

The whole thing was giving Carissa a headache. They were watching the video at 1.5x speed, the overhead lights in the room were stale and florescent, and Jess smelled kind of bad because she'd skipped the post-squash shower in favor of studying. It was one of those soft headaches that seeped down through her body. It made her thighs feel heavy as her legs dangled off the bed.

Grace complained about how hot the laptop was getting. The next video up was about slavery; it'd have the same cartoon-ish graphics.

Jess announced she was going to shower, finally, and with much effort stood up off the floor and left.

What happened next was all a bit of a blur. Carissa was done studying, done basking in the shittiness of it. A spark of energy hit her. She nudged Grace and nodded toward the window. They threw on their jackets and opened the door quickly. Grace jumped down the stairs two at a time (Carissa, one at a time), and finally they thrust the door open against the wind and set off into the cold, dark December air. It was only until after they were outside and walking that Carissa realized Sarah wasn't with them.

"Where are we going?" Carissa asked, her breath scattering around her face.

Grace didn't respond. They both had their backpacks on, something Carissa only realized then.

She felt hungry, a feeling she wished would come over her when she actually went to the dining hall to eat. When the food was right in front of her, she could hardly eat a bite, regardless of how hungry she was. She was thinking of this when her phone started to ring, or vibrate.

*Brother Moraine*

"Hello," Carissa said, tucking the top of her phone inside her gray beanie.

"What's going on, Carizzle?"

"Not much, just walking around, clearing the head and all. Exams are coming up."

"It's cold out, ain't it?" Alex said. *Maury* said. "I just got home, if you can call it that. Home is like five minutes away from campus."

"Damn, college lets out early."

"Yep. Well I still have one final left, it's a paper. It's not due for another couple of days. Say, Rizz-o, you wouldn't happen to know anything about the short stories of Raymond Carver?"

"Who?"

"My thoughts exactly. I've got to write a ten pager on one of his short stories." Alex laughed again, the kind of hearty laugh he always threw out when he was being self-deprecating. "I've gotta write ten fuckin' pages on a story that's only six pages. You know, if there's one thing I wish St. D's prepared me for, it'd be that you actually have to *read* in college. The professors all pick books that aren't on SparkNotes."

"Why are you taking an English class?" Carissa asked, knowing her brother was planning on majoring in Biology. "And is six pages really too much to ask for?"

"Liberal Arts hocus pocus. Same reason I'm in a Gender Studies class. And yes, I'll have you know, six pages is six too many pages when you're trying to live as large as I do."

Grace motioned to Carissa that they'd take a detour across The Lawn.

"You know," Alex continued, "it would've really helped for my final in that Gender Studies class if you'd told me what this whole feminism thing is about."

Carissa laughed, though she didn't want to. "You're the worst," she said.

"Hey, I'm the one calling to check in on you! Tell me, lil' sis, what's a-hap-hap-*happening* at the old STD these days?"

"What do you mean?"

"I mean how are the youngins in your grade holding up? You know, Birdie, Mark, the Toddster, those guys?"

Grace looked over at Carissa. She totally heard Alex say Mark's name over the phone.

"Umm…" Carissa began, unsure what to say. "They're good, I guess." Should she tell Alex that she was in the process of getting to actually be friends with them?

"Ah, never mind. You were never really that close with them. Tryna stay away from me and my crowd and all, I get it."

"Hey, it wasn't— "

"I'm just messing with you, Carrie. Anyway what's the word on campus? Any juicy gossip?"

Alex always seemed above it when he was at St. D's, the rumors and all the bullshit. But he'd always fill Carissa in on the latest gossip during breaks. Maury and Alex were quite different people it seemed.

"Well," Carissa said. She and Grace were nearing the AC. "Do you remember Steven Moriarti?"

"Weird kid in your grade?"

"Close, grade above me. He just got expelled after it was somehow leaked that he was the owner of some meme page on Instagram. Apparently he posted some real, uh, *spicy* memes."

"What page?"

"ShrekNuts3000"

"No way!"

Carissa didn't need to follow up on that one. She moved on: "And yeah also some freshman girl in my dorm hooked up with a senior."

"Who?"

"You wouldn't know her, she's a freshman."

"The senior, Rizzy. The senior."

"I'm not sure, to be honest." That was a lie.

"Oh. Bummer. Anything else?"

"I don't know, hold on," Carissa said. She thought to ask Grace, but noticed that Grace was no longer walking next to her. She was seated at a bench about fifty feet back, right by the door of the AC. Carissa called out, "Grace!"

"Who?"

Grace waved Carissa toward her. "Never mind," she said. "Oh actually, I'm with Grace Martin. You know, Mark's girlfriend?"

"Really? Huh."

Carissa was by Grace's bench now, hovering over her. "Grace," she began, "know any good gossip Alex, err, *Maury* would like to know about?"

Grace, after some thought, which really left Alex awkwardly on the line probably, eventually referenced some old gossip.

"Oh yeah," Carissa repeated to her brother. "There's some rumor going around that Mr. McMahon was drugged on the first day of school."

"Whataaaat?" Alex said, in an obviously feigned tone of disbelief.

"I don't know, he passed out in my English class on the first day of school. Apparently doesn't remember anything."

"I wouldn't know anything about that," he said, failing to hold back laughter.

"What do you know?" Carissa asked passionately, expecting to rile Grace. She looked at her friend on the bench and saw she was crying.

"Listen, mi *Corazon*, I don't know anything about anything. That's hilarious though. Fuck that guy."

Yeah, Grace was crying. If she was trying to hide it at first, she'd definitely realized Carissa had been looking at her funny and was now really just letting the sobs and sighs out.

"Listen, Alex, I gotta go."

"Alright, I was just calling to wish you well on your finals. Good luck lil' sis. Don't do anything stupid now. Looking forward to seeing you in a week!"

Carissa hung up without saying goodbye, which she immediately regretted.

"Gracie! What's wrong?" she said in an affectedly high pitched register. She also immediately regretted calling Grace *Gracie*, something she'd never done before.

Grace didn't really say anything. She was then trying to get in breaths between sobs. Her cries were unsettling to say the least. Maybe because it was Grace, and Grace wasn't the kind of person to cry—ever—or maybe it was because they were in a quasi-public space, but the whole ordeal was just really embarrassing.

She eventually just handed Carissa her phone, which was already unlocked. The screen was wet with tears. It was her texts with Mark, and Carissa wasn't quite sure how far she should scroll up. She peeked up a little bit, and the texts were:

Mark: I'm just going to be busy winter break! I don't think we can see each other! Are u really trying to get in the way of my family?

Grace: Of course I'm not sweetheart I just want to see you.

Grace: I'm sorry.

Mark: Well don't make me feel bad about it.

Mark: I'm sorry I can't see you but like what do you want me to do?

Grace: I just want you to show you still love me every once and a while.

Mark: What does that even mean?

Grace: Like I don't know you just don't really show your love anymore.

Mark: Really? Cuz I can list out all the times over the past couple of months that I very clearly showed my love for you.

Grace: Well that's not the point I'm not saying you don't show your love I'm just saying how I feel.

Grace: Could you tell me again what you love about me?

Mark: I don't know what it will take to convince you that I love you.

Grace: I just am feeling kind of sad and want to hear what you love about me.

Mark: That's not fair.

Mark: Forget it.

Mark: Nothing's ever enough.

Mark: What do you want me to say?

Grace: Nevermind. I'm sorry.

Mark: Stop being sorry, goddamnit.

Mark: I love you.

Grace: But why?

Mark: Jesus hon.

Mark: I'm going to study with Chris. I can't focus when you keep asking me unfair questions like this.

Grace was just sniffling by the time Carissa finished reading the messages.

"Oh, Grace," Carissa said, handing her back her phone and putting her arm around her.

"I just don't know," Grace said, trailing off, trying for another sob which wouldn't come.

"Shh, shh…" Carissa patted her on the head. "Hey, you know, boys are just the worst sometimes. But I know he loves you. You know he loves you too. And you're not wrong. And he's being an ass. And we're all just really stressed out right now, with finals and everything. But you're the best. There's so much to love about you. Just look at us! I have absolutely *loved* getting to know you these past couple of months. You rock, girl. You're the best. And Mark doesn't mean wrong, he's definitely just as stressed as all of us."

Regardless of how Grace took that little pep-talk, she'd stopped crying. At least, she'd stopped crying audibly. She wiped her eyes and said something along the lines of "Thank you," and declared she was just being silly and that, yeah, Carissa was right. Grace then said she just needed to go home and shower, that it was getting late.

Carissa oftentimes wished that Grace lived on campus. Tonight was not one of those nights. By the time she and Grace hugged and Grace left, Carissa was already hating herself for being thankful that Grace could just fuck off like that. And then, logically, she began to hate herself for even remotely taking Mark's side. He was being an absolute *cunt*, which was a word Carissa was surprised to have pop in her head. But it was true. And well then, but so like *why* was Carissa feeling out both sides of the argument? To comfort Grace? No. If Carissa really wanted to comfort Grace she would've said outright that Mark was being a *cunt*, letting Grace be as surprised as her to hear that word. Then they'd laugh. And hug. And they'd both go back to Carissa's room and eat Wheat Thins and talk about anything other than schoolwork and Mark.

But Carissa played both sides, obviously to Grace's detriment, for reasons Carissa laughed out loud at for even remotely trying to suppress in her head. And didn't she look the fool, laughing alone on a dark bench by the AC? To think she'd been embarrassed just moments before to be next to Grace while she was crying about genuinely heart-fucking stuff. Yeah, Carissa said what she'd said because she wanted Grace to stay with Mark because that was her best shot at getting in with Birdie. Of dating Birdie. Of hooking up with him, kissing him, fucking him. Hell, of *marrying* him.

So had she only become friends with Grace to get closer, transitively, to Birdie? Of course not. She wasn't that smart, or that cruel. Was it a miracle that she had become close with Grace? Sure. Did she sometimes consciously try and change her whole persona such that it'd let her get closer with Grace? Maybe. Birdie once said "*What even is being yourself?*"

Despite her worst intentions, though, that thought couldn't really sit easily in Carissa's mind. She desperately wanted to agree philosophically with Birdie, because then they'd have so much in common. But Carissa couldn't help herself from wondering who *herself* was. And more importantly, Carissa couldn't help but wonder if she was a good person.

Carissa was more than aware that it was the general campus consensus that she was a good person, but also deep down feared that this was simply because she was hot and didn't talk much. What's more, she knew and could finally recognize the thing she suffered from, which was, like, probably something along the lines of what one might call depression. And it was hard to think about anything other than herself because she didn't know if she could accept the fact that she *might* be a bad person while also accepting the fact that she, like, had some sort of depression. Because if she ever started to hate herself then she'd think it was the depression talking, but if she ever blamed her shitty behavior on her depression then it'd crush her. And if she ever was crushed she'd start acting like a bad person and if she ever started acting like a bad person…

Carissa screamed, loud and untethered. Nothing, no one heard her.

///Birdie never really studied for anything, being Birdie and all. He had the dorm practically to himself, with everyone out and about cramming for their upcoming finals. So he sat with his guitar and ripped his Juul and fell into another bout of creativity, strumming and picking and desperately trying to think of lyrical refrains that didn't suck. The best one he could think of that night, perhaps the best one he'd ever managed to think of, was the line "And if you think we're a-smarter / well I a-know we ain't / 'Cause there's a-no such thing / as a teenage saint."

# SEVEN

# SUNDAY, APRIL 14TH, 2019. 11:18 PM.

———

Harvard parties reminded Maury of St. D's dances, but with freely flowing booze. Inside, all of his new friends were grinding and jumping and swaying, and he could hear the thumping of some EDM bop from the other side of the stairwell's metal door. Two doors down on the right. If Maury wanted to he could just walk up and submerge himself back into the party. "The Roaring '20s" was the party's theme with everyone dressed like either Gatsby or Daisy. Only Maury and his buddies had called it "The Whoring '20s," because, well, you know.

Tomorrow was Patriots Day.

And he really thought about it, just heading back up to the party. He'd come back to check on her in a little bit, bring her some water. She'd be alright.

Who even was she, like, anyway? They'd been hooking up for a couple of months now, and so what now they were like a thing? Maury tried to flex his temples and recollect her middle name. Her name was Cheryl Craven, which Maury always thought was cute in an antiquated sort of way. Like, *Hey everybody, it's the old-timers Maurice and Cheryl!* Only Maury's name wasn't Maurice, was it?

His body got warm, really warm. It must've been his jacket. He was overheating. Cheryl's head was heavy in his hands. He sat with his back awkwardly pressed against the side of the bottom step. His girl lay kind of stupidly with her legs up a couple steps, her head resting in Maury's hands. If someone were to come down the steps just then, they'd like totally get to see up Cheryl's little sporty skirt. Did she even care?

That's why Maury wasn't really sure if he loved her. It always seemed like she could slip through his fingers if a bigger, prettier, smarter guy came around. The way she kind of opened herself up at parties, not really wanting to dance with Maury or anything, or even be seen with him. Until, of course, the party ended, and they'd go back to Maury's room to fuck.

A memory popped into Maury's mind, although it was all fragmented and fizzy. He couldn't really think straight, and the crimson staircase railing was starting to twirl like a baton. Anyway the memory—or was he dreaming?—involved some kid that could fly saying how he was going to make some old man collapse, and *this* was how he was going to do it.

The memory then shifted to somewhere with swing music and flashing lights. Maury guessed it must be the same place where all that sound was coming from upstairs. Maury's taking a little white pill, looking at Cheryl across the dance floor (which was really the linoleum floor of some sophomore's dorm room), and she's talking with some guy who's probably three inches taller than Maury.

Now he was really burning up in the stairwell, and he felt one of his testicles falling asleep under the weight of his hands and Cheryl's head. He didn't even think it was possible for a ball to get those pins and needles. His eyes had been closed for some time because of the spins. He lifted Cheryl's head up and kind of pushed it over toward his knees, a motion which let his nuts breathe but kind of like caused Cheryl's body to slide down the stairs. It didn't make the thumping sound on each step as Maury expected; instead her head just slipped silently across his lap until he was cradling her in his arms.

Maury wanted to take his jacket off, because he was *seriously* hot now, but he couldn't really—because of the body he was holding.

They'd been fighting, obviously. But then what happened?

"Yo, Alex!" Someone called from above, which was weird because Maury couldn't remember hearing someone open up that gargantuan metal door. Had he passed out?

"Yo!" he called back, eyes still closed, head rocking side to side.

"You all good man?"

"Yaaaaa!" he answered, holding out the *aaa* sound until he lost his breath.

"Shit man, you don't look so good!" came a voice that sounded black. Which like totally didn't matter, obviously, but like still come on it wasn't his fault for like recognizing that. What had he said?

"You sure you don't need some help?" said a different voice, squeakier.

Maury opened his eyes half expecting to be looking down at himself. It was weird. As soon as he opened his eyes, the first sensory information that registered was olfactory. It stunk. *Olfactory*, that was one of Mr. McMahon's favorite words.

"She doesn't look okay, man. You sure you got this?" came a fourth voice from above, with what sounded like a French accent.

Maury looked down at the limp body in his arms.

"All good, bro!" he finally responded. Then he heard the metal doors open and shut, sending a massive echo throughout the stairwell.

"Aight, Cheryl, let's get up." He tried to prop her up against the railing, and even though she couldn't weigh more than 120 pounds, she was putting up quite the fight. Only it wasn't her that was fighting. It was gravity.

He finally got her slouched across from him, her head resting against a thin lower handrail, which actually didn't seem to serve any function at all unless there were like midgets in the dorm or something. Or was it dwarves? He couldn't remember which was derogatory.

He was parsing out the word *imp* internally when Cheryl slumped sideways onto the gray rubber stair treads. Her head smacked against the corner of the second step. "Okay, Cheryl, let's stop fucking around now," he said. The crimson railings in front of him began to spin again, so he reached forward and grabbed onto it to support himself. Then everything happened at once, although it really must have happened in some sort of order, although that order would never reveal itself to his memory.

His hands were covered in blood, as was the red railing. Although it was hard to tell the railing was bloody because, you know, Harvard Crimson. Blood dripped down the steps, going *drip drip*, echoing through the stairwell. Although maybe it was just echoing through Maury's mind. Cheryl, well, she wasn't really in the mood for talking. Or responding. And one of them had evidently pissed themselves, maybe both of them had, at some point or another. And Maury realized he still had, like, an eighth of a boner sometime in there as well.

Then a sound pierced through Maury's ears, a harsh *thud*. He looked around, but nothing was moving. And the sound wasn't echoing. And then again, another *thud*. And another, louder. He closed his eyes and saw Cheryl falling down the stairs, landing with that *thud*. And he looked down, his eyes still closed, and saw his hands. He had pushed her.

His ears were ringing, and when he opened his eyes he found that he'd thrown up, mostly all over Cheryl. Maury wasn't a doctor, but he was pretty sure Cheryl was dead. And so that phrase, *Cheryl is dead*, looped in his mind, obstructing any other thought. He couldn't think to like check her pulse or anything, or see if she was breathing. He'd decided, or somehow just realized, that Cheryl was dead.

Cheryl was dead.

The thought, after several dozen repetitions in his mind, became a fact. Not only a fact, but a reassuring one at that. It was unfortunate that Cheryl was dead, but hey, what could he do? Cheryl was dead. It almost calmed him, if you could call it calm. He found solace in the phrase, as if it explained the whole situation. It was a relief to be so sure that Cheryl was dead.

So Maury stood up, with some effort. The first time he tried to get up, he'd used the railing as a support, but it was quite slippery and he couldn't really grip it well so he fell back down on his ass. The jolt of pain snapped him out of the *Cheryl is dead* loop, and he used the wall to get himself vertical. Stepping over Cheryl (as well as the now sizable pool of blood at the base of the steps), Maury leaped up the steps two at a time. He was feeling good. He was hammered, but energized.

The door was heavier than he remembered, until he realized it was push not pull.

Two doors down on the right, the music was still blasting. Colorful lights flashed from the slit under the door. He opened it and walked in, dancing in step to what he could then recognize as "Mr. Brightside."

People were yelling behind him as he grabbed a solo cup and poured himself wine from a box. Was somebody shotgunning a beer? He turned to see what was up, but everyone was moving around so quickly. His vision was blurry. He thought about how hungover he was going to be the next morning.

People were staring at him, but he didn't mind the attention. He was used to it. He always turned heads whenever he entered the dining hall at St. D's. He was a presence in whatever room he occupied. Big man on campus.

Some chick threw up right on the god damn linoleum right god damn in front of him. He smoothly stutter-stepped and shimmied around the drunken girl and patted her on the back with his free hand as he did so.

The dance floor was crowded, and the song was almost over. Maury shoved through some bodies with his hands above his head, spilling a bit of wine he guessed because someone said "What the fuck," in a not-so-friendly tone as he passed by. Over by the window on the far side of the room was that tall handsome guy Cheryl had been flirting with earlier. It seemed so silly to Maury now, that he'd been so mad about that. Maybe it was the booze talking, but he felt like he needed to go apologize to that guy for hating him without even, like, getting the chance to know him.

The big guy was talking with some other girl who looked nothing like Cheryl when Maury finally got near. The big guy looked up and down at Maury in disgust.

"Hey man," Maury said, trying to put his arm around the big guy's shoulder. He wasn't in the mood for that, or something, because he shrank away. Whatever. "Hey, look, I'm sorry, but like I hated you earlier tonight for no good reason. We should get to know each other."

The big guy just stared at Maury, dumbstruck. The girl he was with had vanished.

"Hello?" Maury waved his hand in front of the big guy's face. "I'm talking to you!"

The big guy fell hard to the ground, like a tree. Maury looked around to see if anyone else saw what he was seeing, but the room was empty.

"Lame party," he said. He grabbed a blanket from the bed next to him and laid it over the big guy. "Why don't you just get some rest there buddy."

He guessed the party was moving someplace else, and those dummies had left a good amount of booze behind. Maury danced alone to the next song, another throwback in Sean Kingston's "Fire Burning," for a verse and a chorus before finishing what was left of the wine straight from the box and exiting the room.

In the hall, some girl was rocking back and forth, in a ball. A friend was trying to comfort her, probably some bad acid trip or something. She had a red handprint on her back.

"Stop right there!" A voice boomed from down the hall. It was campus police, come to bust the party. That explained why everyone was out in such a hurry. He thought about booking it, but another officer emerged from the stairwell on the left. The officer was crying, as was the girl on the floor.

///Meanwhile, fifty miles east, Mark was experiencing another re-trip, rocking back and forth on his bed as softly as he could, trying not to wake Birdie.///

# THE FIRST DAY OF SCHOOL. 8:11 PM.

———

Frank walked into Mark and Birdie's room just as Mark was heading out. Birdie and Todd were seated on the futon.

"Grace is totally in the top three now," they said in unison, not acknowledging Frank's presence.

"Dude, like when are we gonna stop talking about this shit, man?" Birdie asked Todd, without so much as a wave to Frank.

"Bird-dog," Todd said, "I think it's simple: we live in an environment, right, that like totally leaves us with nothing to do but abstractly think about *the other,* the other being the females on campus. Cause they live in different dorms and do different shit and have boobs and the like." Todd, his eyes all red and squinty, turned and briefly looked at Frank. "But on the other hand, right, more generally, we're just constantly exposed to beautiful women on Instagram and Facebook and that thingy *TikTok* and YouTube and Pornhub, right? So how the fuck else can we like how can we think of anything *other than* the beautiful women in our grade?"

Birdie nodded.

"And *furthermore*," Todd stood up as he said this, "we are raised in an educational system whereby we receive letter grades assessing not only our performance, but in a larger sense out *worth*. Call an 'F' a zero and an 'A+' a ten. We internalize this shit, man. That's why there are power ranking for football teams, that's why we ask each other what our top five Kanye songs are, our top three movies *et fucking cetera,* and ultimately it just like makes too much sense that we inevitably ask each other who the three hottest girls in our grade are!"

"But you didn't answer my question," Birdie said, still seated.

"Well if it wasn't transitively obvious from my spiel there, then to answer your question: I don't know when you'll stop entertaining notions of 'who are the top three hottest girls in our grade' will be. But I know for sure that it's not your fault for thinking it, as much as it isn't mine!"

And this all kind of obviously went over Frank's head, because as soon as he caught wind of what it was they'd been discussing, he immediately began to wonder what *his* personal top-three hottest girls in the grade were. And, more importantly, whether or not Sarah made the cut.

Mark walked back in, shaking his hands free of either piss or faucet water. Because whenever Frank shook his hands after taking a piss, he wasn't shaking off faucet water. But maybe, and perhaps probably, Mark was the kind of chap who actually made a point to wash his hands after he peed.

"Hey guys," Frank began. "I was thinking…"

And this was usually where someone—Birdie—would interrupt him. But Birdie looked like he was entrenched in some philosophical mental conundrum after hearing Todd's words. No one really seemed to be paying attention, so maybe Frank would have to repeat his thoughts again after he said them. But hey, it was a good idea he was about to put forth. It was a *Birdie* idea.

"I was thinking we go up and introduce ourselves to the freshmen," Frank proposed.

"Yeah sure," said Todd, his phone having materialized in his hand.

"You know, Todd," Birdie said. He was totally about to derail Frank's suggestion. "I was telling Mark earlier, we oughtta call the freshmen the Toddlers, them being young and naive, and you being on their floor and being named Todd and all."

Everyone laughed, Frank included.

"Sure," Mark added, but by then it was a done deal. They were already on their way upstairs, with Todd running up in an affected high-knee style.

Frank asked Todd which room they should congregate in; Todd pointed to the one double on the floor. Two pieces of burnt orange construction paper were taped onto the door, one reading BEN STEINER!, and the other *miles maloney* in a feminine cursive.

"I'll get the others," Todd said. He set off, banging on freshmen doors.

Birdie knocked on the door to the double, *duh duh duh-duh duh, duh duh.* A muffled but high-pitched "come in" came from inside, but Birdie was already turning the doorknob. Frank followed Birdie.

Inside were four boys. A pimple-faced kid sat on a bed, swinging his legs. A gangly, tall fella with hair down to his shoulders leaned against a desk, wearing a tie-dye shirt. One shirtless boy was folding laundry into a dresser. He had more chest hair than Frank. The last kid, who Frank recognized as Miles from football practice, was hanging up Christmas lights from the ceiling's four corners.

"I couldn't find them," Todd said as he entered behind Frank. "Oh."

The hairy one ended up being the one and only BEN STEINER!. The pimply one introduced himself as Eli, but said that people had already started calling him "Go-Go," because of something about his last name. Hippie Jesus said his name was Chester, which made the other freshmen laugh. Some inside joke, or something.

Mark and Birdie did their classic introduction where they introduce themselves as the other. This time the overly eager, already annoying Go-Go said to Mark, "You *totally* look like a Birdie!"

Frank thought it'd be funny if he introduced himself as Todd, only BEN STEINER! commented on there being two Todds.

"I'm Frank, just messing with you. Sorry," he said, wiping his mouth and leaning against the door.

The freshmen chatted amongst themselves. Their confidence in the presence of upperclassmen was jarring and upsetting. It was as if he and Todd and the other guys weren't even there. It made Frank feel like an intruder. Eventually, everybody in the room was on their phones. Frank just swiped back and forth on his home screen, having no one to text, no Instagram posts to see, no games to play. He'd deleted all the games on his phone the other day, worried he'd spent too much time staring at a screen.

Frank had Dion's "Runaround Sue" stuck in his head and imagined everyone in the room breaking into song and dance, swaying and bobbing, smiling and snapping their fingers in time. Frank singing lead. Of course, it was Birdie that looked more like a young Dion DiMucci, not Frank. The whole fantasy was pretty fucking gay anyway.

"So," Frank said quietly and garnered only a pair of raised eyes from the nearby BEN STEINER!. He cleared his throat, then began more loudly, perhaps overcompensatingly loud, "So what did you guys, uh, think about your first day? Any teachers you like? Hate?"

Chester looked over at Go-Go, and mumbled something through a smile that Frank couldn't quite discern. The two freshmen laughed, then went back to their phones.

"Just, I don't know man, it's just school," Miles said. He'd finished hanging up the lights and was digging gunk out of his fingernails with a thumbtack.

"Cool, cool," Frank said.

"School, school," mocked Chester, hardly able to contain his giggles. Go-Go was lying on his back on the bed, having what appeared to be an asthma attack. It was only when he sat up, with noticeable effort, did Frank see that the freshman was laughing so hard he couldn't breathe.

This scene didn't faze Mark or Todd, who were just showing each other memes on their phones. Birdie, however, when Frank got a look at him, was seething.

BEN STEINER! pulled out a Juul and took a rip, carelessly blowing several O's right in the direction of the door. If a faculty member were to walk in, they'd all be rightfully fucked. Frank and the guys especially, being responsible juniors and all.

"Don't do that," Birdie admonished. "And are you kids *high*?"

Chester and Go-Go went belly-up in laughter, Go-Go already halfway there to begin with. BEN STEINER! offered Birdie the Juul, perhaps as amends for committing some wrongdoing he wasn't aware of. Birdie waved it away.

Frank wasn't going to ask the kid for a rip or two, even though if he did ask he'd probably get it in his hands. He hadn't been able to get any nicotine into his system since arriving at St. D's. But he didn't want to let his friends know that he'd totally gotten hooked over the summer. He watched BEN STEINER! flip the Juul around in his fingers, retracting the offer to Birdie. He wondered if maybe the offer would turn to him, although probably not. But maybe. Well, the window of probability closed after BEN STEINER! slid the Juul into his pocket after rubbing it across his hairy chest. The thought of putting it to his mouth, even then, wasn't so unappealing. Frank thought about asking something like "*Is that a Juul?*" to appear as though it wasn't something he was all too familiar with, but curious about. So that maybe BEN STEINER! would pull it back out, say "*Yep, you want some?*" Then Frank could like take a couple of rips, acting like it was his first time, and pretend to cough and say something like "*Yeah, I remember now why we don't do that,*" to appease Birdie. Mark and Todd wouldn't care in the first place. Or Frank could get real chummy with this BEN STEINER! kid, maybe come back up later alone and see what was good and yeah also could he hit the Juul?

"Frank-o, you coming?" Todd asked, holding the door open. His friends had already left.

"Unbelievable!" Birdie said later. He placed Todd's dab pen on the charger, hidden behind the futon, and exhaled. It smelled like strawberries. "Fucking freshmen, dude."

"You do realize the hypocritical nature of your astonishment," Todd said. He was squatting on Mark's chair with a copy of *Macbeth* flipped open to one of the first pages.

"No, man. I fucking *earned* the right to get high and break the rules. Those kids don't even know what the rules are yet! They haven't even been indoctrinated into the shit-fest that is St. Dominic's! They have no reason to smoke—it's just raw hedonism."

And what did *hedonism* mean, again?

"Relax, Albert," Mark said. That suggestion, combined with the weed doing its thing, mellowed Birdie out. Or at least Birdie didn't say much for a while.

"I've been thinking," Todd began after a few episodes of *Family Guy*, "We should find a way to get booze onto campus."

"Have you ever seen a freshman that hairy?"

"Where's Chris?"

"God I already miss Maury."

Frank was way up inside his own head. Five hits might've been too much to handle, and what was the battery set to anyway? He was staring at a Megan Fox poster on the wall. He couldn't tell who was saying what.

"And that kid…Chester was it?"

"Why does Mark always sleep on the top bunk?"

"McMahon today, you shoulda seen it, it was perfect."

"Of course I've felt them! She's my girlfriend!"

"Would you rather…"

"Have you seen…"

"Top three…"

"What if…"

"Would you ever…"

"Can't believe chest-hair just whipped out the Juul like that."

Frank perked up. "It wasn't Chester, it was BEN STEINER!"

"I said chest-hair, Frankie. Chest. Hair." Birdie clarified. "Anyway I think it's time to hit the hay."

Mark, who was already in bed, concurred. How much time had passed?

"Looks like it's just you and me, Frank," Todd said. "Wanna go back to my room?"

Todd's room was right next to BEN STEINER!'s, and it was only 10:31 so BEN STEINER! would probably still be awake. Maybe Frank could pretend like he was missing his own Juul, and did he leave it in there? Put on a show, look around where he'd been standing. And then maybe BEN STEINER! would say something like, "B*ummer bro, hey do you want a rip of mine?*" and then Frank could ask apprehensively

"*What flavor?*" as if it mattered. Then he could pretend to be relieved with whatever flavor BEN STEINER! answered with because that was Frank's favorite flavor, and thank God BEN STEINER! didn't have that *other* flavor in there. So then Frank would casually take a long rip and ask him a personal question while he exhaled. Because maybe BEN STEINER! was the type to keep a close eye on his Juul when he gave it away, so a dummy question would give Frank enough time to take another long rip while he answered. Then if BEN STEINER! motioned for Frank to return the Juul, Frank could get in another cheeky rip before handing back the vape and saying, "*Thank you BEN STEINER!*"

Three good rips over thirty seconds would be enough to get Frank's head spinning and buzzing and spinning and buzzing and spinning and...

///*Before bed, Todd sent Henry a quick little text, feeling happy and high: Hey, Henry the Eighth (get it?), thanks for the weeeeed!!!///*

# TUESDAY, AUGUST 13TH, 2019. 11:10 AM.

———

Once again, Sarah was in the shower. Although she couldn't stay for long this time. She'd overslept by about two hours and had to get ready. She was going to meet Carissa for lunch in an hour, and it was at least a forty-five minute drive to Cambridge.

The water was a bit too hot, exactly the way she liked it.

Dorm assignments for the seniors had just been released. This year, she wasn't rooming with Carissa. In fact, they were on different floors. Carissa got the honor of being a Senior Proctor, so she'd be with all the freshmen.

And it was really almost senior year, which meant it was really almost time for Sarah to give her chapel. Assuming she got approved to give one. Only twenty-two spots. Usually only twenty-five seniors tried to give one anyway, so her odds were good. Unless the administration somehow held something against Sarah and didn't want her to give a chapel because, even though they say it's randomly selected, it's pretty unlikely you'll get denied if you've got straight A's or play a varsity sport. Sarah got an A in history last year, she was proud of that. Otherwise, B's.

She never even made a JV team—not that she tried or cared.

She'd set an alarm on her phone to make sure she was out of the shower within seven minutes, giving her enough time to dry off, pick out an outfit, find her car keys, ask her dad for twenty bucks, and get to Carissa's only five minutes late. Two minutes had probably already gone by.

Sarah had the beginning of her chapel already memorized in her head. Most every time she took a shower, she repeated it aloud, softly, then tried to add to it.

"*When I arrived at St. Dominic's,*" she said to the rubber duck on the soap tray, "*I wore incredibly, shall I say, modest clothes—baggy jeans, dresses covering the ankles, things that any father wishes their daughter would wear.*" Pause for laughter. "*Before I arrived at St. Dominic's, I had never gotten below an A- in any class, I'd never been to a football game, I'd never seen a rated R movie, and I'd never kissed a boy.*"

She grabbed the rubber ducky and gave it a kiss on the lips, something she'd started doing after that part about two weeks ago. It was unlikely she'd bring the duck onstage when it was showtime, but who knew.

*"Let's just say my freshman year was not what I expected. I got a B, which was whatever. I went to a football game, which we lost. I saw a rated R movie,* The Conjuring, *which gave me nightmares for weeks."* Pause again for laughter, she's killing it. *"And I kissed a boy, and he told everyone he knew that we did a lot more than just kiss."* Dramatic pause. Only, this was as far as she had memorized, so the dramatic pause lasted quite a while.

She figured she only had a minute or two left before the alarm went off, so washing and conditioning her hair was out of the question.

*"Poor old me,"* she continued, in a softer voice. *"Yes, poor old me. You know what else poor old me did, Mr. Duck? Poor old me asked Chris for a fucking N-word pass!"*

The alarm went off. Her sense of time must have been thrown off by the quick piss she'd taken before getting in the shower.

*"Poor old me got a reputation for being that slutty freshman girl, but poor old me spread more rumors about other bitches than were spread about me!"*

Those alarms can be so insistent, like *Hey! Hey! You haven't said no yet! I'm just gonna keep on a-ringin'!*

If Sarah ever decided to talk about the third time she hooked up with the fourth boy she'd hooked up with, maybe that'd be a good analogy.

"And if it wasn't for fucking Carissa Moraine, I would've trans-ferred. Hell, I'd told my parents I wanted out by the end of freshman year."

She wondered how long the alarm would ring if she never turned it off. Would it ring forever? Or would it eventually give up?

"But you know what, guys?"

She pinched the duck's lips and voiced *What's that, Sarah?*

"Being friends with Carissa Moraine turned out to be a lot of fucking work! She's just an absolute fucking bummer to be around most of the time, and I don't know if I can keep cheering her up forever!"

The alarm kept on ringing.

"I'm gonna be late for our lunch! And you know what? That's gonna make her feel like shit! I know it! If I show up ten min-utes late, she's going to be sitting there for ten minutes thinking that not even her best friend really cares about her!"

Sarah's stomach growled. The water didn't even feel hot anymore.

"You know I care about you, right Mr. Duck?"

She made the duck nod.

"*And you don't make me prove it to you every second of every day, right?*"

She made the duck shake its head.

"*So tell me, Mr. Duck, how long is that fucking alarm gonna keep ringing? Should I wait for it to turn itself off? Will it even turn itself off? The battery's gotta die at some point. But the alarm should have some fucking feature to turn itself off after it's been made abundantly fucking clear that its goddamn owner isn't going to satisfy it, or recognize it, or thank it for waking them up!*"

She squeezed the duck. The duck squealed back at her until it was re-inflated. She did this again, and the duck kept screaming. After a while, the alarm did turn itself off.

///*Sarah showed up twenty minutes late to Carissa's house, but Carissa said it was, like, totally fine because she had to shower and stuff anyway.*///

# THE FIRST FRIDAY OF SUMMER. 11:29 PM.

———

Todd was leaning over the back of the couch, face next to Birdie's, and Birdie was giving him instructions to find the Juul charger and the pods, which would be in the other house. Then Birdie stopped talking and Todd felt a bit dizzy. Perhaps Birdie's steady and direct instructions had been anchoring Todd to the precariously balanced position he was in, leaning over the back of the couch. The silence was *definitely* now making him a bit nauseous, but he had to say something to let Birdie know he was indeed up for the task, even if he wasn't, really, so he said, "Bed. Underwear. Yep." in as sobering a tone as he could muster. Then Birdie was patting his head like a dog which he took as his cue to up and leave, so Todd heaved himself back off the couch and twirled around, less of a body-nausea now with two feet on the ground as much as it was a head-nausea. The room was spinning and all that, but so as to let Birdie know that he was indeed up for the task, even if he wasn't, really, he said, "I'll be back 'fore you know it," and began to, as silently as he could (this was a stealth mission, after all), muster his way across the kitchen-ette without stumbling into anything, which would be bad, and slipped out the door, careful not to let the screen door smack into the doorframe, which it did sometimes.

Outside the grass was wet and Todd had forgotten to put on his sneakers before leaving, so he did a sort of startled high-knees for several paces as a reactionary measure. His stride switched to a sort of light-on-his-feet stealth move—continuing long after his socks had become fully soaked past where most people would just cut their losses—and splashed through the wet grass. He was halfway across the lawn separating the guest house from the main house. And to set the record straight, he *had* considered walking on the presumably drier gravel driveway but opted against it out of fear of stepping on a particularly sharp rock and reflexively hollering, blowing his cover. He then began to wonder why the grass was so wet on such a starry night when a sprinkler head reared its ugly face in the darkness (Todd imagined this, after the fact) and sputtered to a start, spraying Todd head-on (more like belly-on).

Forced then to vacate the varying radii of sprinklers (Todd's ass could attest to there being more than one sprinkler), he sought refuge on the gravel driveway. Todd's high-knee-stealth-walk transformed into a stealthless stutter-step as the little fucking rocks were indeed quite fucking sharp, and he banged his elbow against the rearview mirror of a white Mercedes, the one the girls all showed up in, right in the funny bone. So Todd, for the short remainder of his journey to the side-door of the main house, hobbled with quick feet cradling his limp arm and wincing and, wow, quite literally *seething*, which is something he didn't think he'd ever done before. He finally made it to the door, surprised to find himself laughing.

Of course he had to cut his laughing out right away or else he might wake someone up, even though Birdie's parents were all the way inside on the second floor probably blasting a sleeping machine and snoring. Still too risky. What's more, Todd caught a chill as a gust of wind hit him head-on, his shirt soaked through, and so he decided he'd be best served taking it off, just leaving it right there hanging on the unlit lamp post, to dry, while he quickly ran inside to grab the goods.

The side door led to a little mudroom, which bled into the kitchen, a grand old kitchen with hardwood floors and a big fucking island and lots of cabinets and two dishwashers and a big silver steel fridge and a rack of wine bottles and the like. Even though the lights were off, he could see all this through the blue light emanating from the digitalized ovens and microwaves and fridges. No time to dilly-dally, though. The spiral staircase was maybe twenty feet in front of him. Todd dashed toward it, really slid toward it, gliding across the hardwood floor so as to not make any impact-noise. It was silent inside the house aside from the faint refrigerator buzz.

The stairs were carpeted, and as Todd stepped onto the first of at least twenty winding steps, he heard, against that humming fridge, a soft *splash*, like squeezing a sponge. His socks were still on and were *very* much still sopping wet. He peeled them off, slowly, using his gimpy, funny-bone-banged arm to remove the sock and his sound arm to lean against the stair rail to support his swaying weight, and laid the wet brown socks over the rail and proceeded up the stairs bare-foot, shirtless, and silent.

At the end of the hall, which had an oriental runner laid down so he could continue to move quickly and quietly, Todd figured Birdie's room would be on the right, because that's where Birdie and Mark's room had been in relation to the hallway in Lang. So Todd got himself to the door, took a moment to catch his breath, in fact took more than a moment to catch his breath, and looked out the window at the end of the hall over the sprawling lawn which led straight to the beach, all moonlit and damp, and the guest house straight-ahead. He never really felt poor until he hung out with Birdie.

So it was showtime. Todd opened the door, somewhat hes-itantly, as though he expected Birdie to be inside sleeping. Todd had done this once before when he'd borrowed Birdie's Juul charger (and a pod) from Birdie's room after he'd gone to bed, though obviously never told anyone except for Mark who the next day asked, "What the fuck were you doing creeping around my room last night," and Mark probably never told Birdie anyway. Todd creaked open the door, took a step in, and fished around on the nearby wall to find the light switch—which ended up being much lower than he thought any self-respecting light switch would be.

It's funny, the first thought Todd had when the lights came on was *damn, Birdie's got a pink comforter.* And then of course he saw Maud laying on her stomach on the bed, wearing nothing but a pair of white socks, facing away from the door, on her phone which was plugged into an outlet behind her nightstand. A University of Richmond pennant hung next to a St. Dominic's pennant above the bed.

"Ready for round two?" Maud asked, without turning around.

And here, really, there were like (and this isn't much hyperbole) a thousand thoughts rushing through Todd's inebriated mind. Among them that Maud's ass was a bit flatter when she was lying down, that the light switch was in a stupid location, that Richmond and St. D's have the same colors, that maybe if he turned the lights back off he could indeed be ready for round two, that this is what having a girlfriend was like, and that he needed to say or do something fast.

"Nope," was what Todd landed on, and he quickly turned the lights back off and shut the door and turned around and opened what then, surely, must have been Birdie's room and slid inside and shut the door and reached for the light switch—which frustratingly enough was located at a normal height. The massive poster of Megan Fox with Sharpie'd deformities was a familiar sight. This was indeed Birdie's room.

Bed. Underwear. Yep.

The Juul charger wasn't hard to find. It was just plugged into an outlet behind Birdie's nightstand. The room's configuration was a mirror image of Maud's. The pack of pods were in Birdie's underwear drawer, which you know Birdie could have told him was a drawer underneath the bed as part of, like, some trundle sort of thing so that Todd didn't have to rummage through two dressers worth of shirts and pants and shorts and sweaters. In a nearby room a toilet flushed. There were actually two drawers under the bed, one with socks and the other with underwear. Todd looked through the sock drawer first, figuring you know hey maybe it'd actually be in here. There was a white sock at the bottom with something hard inside of it, not a pack of Juul pods from the feel of it, but what could it be? Todd took the sock out and shimmied the large, cylindrical object out from it. The toilet flushed again.

Lo and behold, it was Todd's missing pocket pussy! He knew it was as it had the same Sharpie'd denotation of "NOT YOURS" he'd written on it, funny enough during the Megan Fox deformation session. The joy of locating what he'd figured was long gone faded quickly, though perhaps not as quickly as it should have faded, before the inevitable realization of *holy oh fucking no way.*

He dropped the thing, shuddered, like, absolutely stunned, and thought of how—if at all—he'd confront Birdie about it. He found the Juul pods, which were literally just sitting on top of all of Birdie's underwear in the drawer, and paced around the room. The idea of acknowledging to Birdie what he'd done, what Birdie had done, that is, was beyond horrifying, and honestly, like, Birdie probably wouldn't psychologically recover from being discovered, even if Todd kept it just between them. Imagine if Frank found out. But something had to be done, something which came to Todd in a moment of pseudo-lucidity, as he was still very much indeed still hammered. You don't just take another man's pocket pussy.

Todd took a thumbtack out from a cork board over Birdie's desk and lodged it in the pocket pussy, pointy-end up, then secured the sex toy back in its *(oh god)* crusty sock, and left the room.

Luckily nothing had come from Maud's room that whole time, and the lights were still off. Maybe he'd done an impressive Nick. Maybe it's like a thing that Nick has, like, bad bowels or something and sometimes just needs to return to the bathroom to finish the job, or something, or maybe Maud was just *really* drunk and hadn't given it too much thought it the first place. Light beamed up the spiral staircase from downstairs. Todd was less deliberately stealthy on his return, having already secured the goods. The worst that could happen now was he bumps into Mr. Fayter in the kitchen or something and, like, why would Mr. Fayter care what Todd was doing anyway?

He grabbed his socks from the rail (they hadn't dried much) and proceeded to quite literally bump into Nick, who was likewise shirtless, carrying two wine glasses and a bottle he'd doubtlessly secured from the wine rack.

"Is that you?" Nick asked, pointing to two streaks of wet dirt on the hardwood floor extending from the mudroom to the spiral staircase. "Don't forget to turn the lights off," he said, before heading upstairs.

Cleaning his footprints, or more like foot-trails, was easy enough. He just grabbed a couple of dish towels and got to scrubbing. While he was on his knees, however, after scrubbing the last bit of dirt from the floor, Todd noticed above him a glass cabinet stocked with brown and green and blue and clear glass bottles.

Upon closer examination, it was indeed the finest private liquor cabinet Todd had ever laid eyes on. Tito's, Bombay Sapphire, Jameson, Bulleit Rye, Don Julio, Captain Morgan's, Crown Royal, Raspberry Stoli, Lemon Stoli, Tanqueray…and that was only the first shelf. Todd hardly dared look much higher than that, but of course he stole a glance. He made out a bottle of Johnny Walker Blue, several different scotches still in their cylindrical cases with numbers like '18' and '24' emblazoned on them, and something covered in dust that said Vat 69, which Todd thought was hilarious.

He opened the glass door, flinching at the audible *pop* of the magnet coming free. He grabbed the bottle of Crown Royal, which was about three-quarters full, and shut the cabinet.

A wine glass sat in the sink with just the faintest splash of Red still in it, which Todd washed out and carried with him back to the guest house, almost forgetting to turn off the lights and fully forgetting to grab his shirt, which had fallen off the lamp post and onto the gravel below.

Todd took the liberty of taking a swig or four straight from the bottle in the mudroom before he left.

Mark and Grace were outside leaning against the white Mercedes. For some reason Todd felt compelled to hide the bottle and glass he carried. He didn't do a good job concealing it, like at all, but neither Mark nor Grace said anything. Instead,

Grace asked "Hey, did you bang your arm against the car earlier? We could've sworn it was you."

To which Todd said, and this was the first thing he'd really tried to say since leaving the guest house in the first place, aside from, "Nope," and come to think of it, it felt like it'd been hours since he embarked on this quest, but anyway, to which he said: "You guys shouldn't get back together," and smiled, and kept walking, doing some sort of acrobatic, serpentine motion through the grass to avoid the sprinklers.

Back inside the guest house, Todd was surprised to be alone. Birdie and Carissa had fucked off somewhere, maybe hooking up. For a moment Todd hoped that Birdie had left the Juul on the coffee table, but then why would Birdie do that? So Todd sat, and poured himself a wineglass of whisky, and slumped down, and took a couple of sips, and opened up the Juul pod and took a sniff, and thought about Maud's ass.

Frank came in at one point from God knows where and asked if he'd seen Sarah, but Todd wasn't really in the business of formulating words, let alone sentences or useful information, so Frank left back to wherever he came from.

By his third glass, Todd had decided that not only was Crown Royal his favorite whisky, *ever*, but that *everyone* should drink whisky out of wineglasses.

His head began to buzz, and he, like, was really starting to need that Juul. And then, speak of the devil himself, Birdie moseyed on down the stairs the way Birdie moseys down stairs.

"Toddster!" Birdie exclaimed, although he didn't sound particularly excited to see Todd. Todd just pinched in the air, a universal signal for *pass me the Juul*, only to remember that it first needed to be charged.

It was nice that Birdie didn't ask about the wineglass or the whisky, which Todd remembered Birdie might freak at him for stealing. He fished through his pocket for the Juul charger, which was small and really buried down there, and felt a bag of something loose in his pocket, which he initially in a moment of panic figured must be somehow someway the pocket pussy he wasn't going to ever bring up, but was instead delighted to discover the bag of Snap Bangs he'd brought. And the Juul charger.

Chris, Jess, and Frank came in a bit later, after the Juul had charged and was being belligerently inhaled by Todd (Birdie surprisingly wasn't really fiending), and they all sat for a bit. Todd threw some Snap Bangs at Frank's feet which Chris thought was funny but Jess was all like *hey Sarah's sleeping upstairs.* Then Frank went upstairs, and Chris and Jess went somewhere, and by then Todd had had a good deal more than three glasses, plus those swigs earlier. After he threw up in the bathroom, he came back and Birdie wasn't even there anymore, and it was just him and the bottle and the wineglass and the Juul which thank God Birdie had left behind. Well, as it turned out the linoleum tile was quite comfortable against Todd's bare skin only someone had left the screen door open a bit, he guessed, 'cause a mosquito buzzed right into his ear, jolting him up, adrenaline providing a bit of level-headedness, level-headedness yielding a sudden memory, a memory of a story, a story Birdie had once told him about this place, this house, and the bottle of Crown Royal was clenched tight in Todd's fist.

///Nick actually did suffer from irritable bowel syndrome (IBS), and it was a bit of private knowledge and respectful patience on Maud's part which allowed Todd to get away with such an unbelievably poor exit strategy.///

# MONDAY, MAY 27TH, 2019. 10:14 AM.

---

"We'd just like to inspect your car, Mr. Dinelli," Dean of Students Mr. Welsh was saying, or something like that.

Henry wasn't really listening. His heart was all, like, in his stomach. It felt like he'd taken too much Adderall, and he didn't know if he needed water or if he was going to throw up or what. It'd be a real bitch to throw up all over himself in his only suit and tie.

He really just should have skipped graduation. Even though it was mandatory, he'd been considering just taking his last unexcused absence of the year. It's not like there were any detentions left. And it's not like Henry had a close relationship with any of the graduating seniors. A couple of them bought from him, sure. But that's not much of a relationship. The only senior Henry ever really actually got along with, Steven Moriarti, got expelled earlier in the year for dumb charges about a meme page on Instagram.

The real kicker to that story, at least how Steven told it, was that he was more or less innocent. Somehow they discovered a bunch of memes from that account attached to his name because of some AirDrop thing that Henry didn't understand. So when they asked Steven if he was the curator of the memes, it should've been a layup to not shit the bed and get expelled. But unfortunately Steven had laughed at just about every meme they showed him, which was incriminating enough. You'd think after three or four dank memes they'd stop showing them to him.

So Henry was being escorted to his car, although not too briskly, because graduation ceremonies were getting underway.

Again, Welsh was on something about "Mrs. Calipari saw you exit your vehicle this morning with what she described as a 'murk of smoke,' you know English teachers and everything."

Welsh had on some stupid St. D's bowtie that he always wore at graduation.

They got to the parking lot, Henry being nudged along like a Kindergartner who has to go apologize for calling someone a *fuckcunt.*

"So, any summer plans?" Welsh asked, as cheerily as if Henry wasn't about to get absolutely bopped.

"You know…," Henry said, for the millionth time, "just beefing up the ol' college resume." The present circumstance cast a dark shadow over the rehearsed response, a darkness which made them both smirk.

They were about five cars away from Henry's piece of shit-colored Subaru, and with X-Ray vision he could see the empty Juul pods, the full Juul pods, the disposable vapes, the medicine bottles filled with THC cartridges, the medicine bottles filled with weed (proper bud), the mushrooms in a little Ziploc baggie, the baking soda that looked an awful lot like cocaine that Henry was going to try and flip to some of the graduating seniors. And, if he squinted, he could faintly make out the cut-out photo of Carissa from last year's yearbook stashed away in the Driver's Manual. What a fucking stupid thing for him to have.

Three cars now separated them from certain doom. Henry pulled out his keys from his too-tight dress pants to unlock the Subaru, which he did.

And then Henry booked it for the car, with Welsh only able to utter out an, "Uhhhh," before Henry was in the car and slamming the door and starting the engine and locking the doors and looking behind him to make sure he wasn't about to slam into Welsh. He pulled out, whipped the wheel around, and kicked it into drive with Welsh banging comedically on the back of the car before he sped off. He didn't slow down for speed bumps and ran right through the stop sign before the campus exit. Teachers and faculty ran after him—he could see them in the rearview mirror. Dozens of them. And students, too, cheering him on, coming at him on the left-hand side from the fields. And Henry revved his engine as some faculty members fell over because they were running faster than their old bodies could carry them. He revved the engine again, students all cheering, those graduating all throwing their caps into the air. Carissa flashed him and blew him a kiss. Then he turned right out of there and zipped off into a never-ending sunset.

Forty-five minutes later, Henry's mom and dad were with him in the Health Center. Not because Henry had any sort of medical emergency, but because the Health Center was where they brought kids before they expelled them. Who knows why. So they sat there, not saying much, as if Henry was awaiting the results from a strep-throat test.

The seniors didn't even wear caps at graduation.

Welsh had confiscated just enough to expel Henry. Once he got his hands on the weed, he didn't think to look for anything else. And the picture of Carissa, well he obviously didn't look through the Driver's Manual.

Welsh walked in after about another half hour, this time with the head of school, Dunks, and Henry's advisor, Mr. Gourd. The advisor was supposed to be there to make the expulsion go down easier, the *spoonful of sugar*, but Henry didn't give much of a rat's ass about Gourd. Gourd, who was as satisfyingly fat as his name would suggest, seemed to loath ever talking with Henry about Henry's feigned passion for Dungeons and Dragons. Henry had never played "D&D," as he called it, but knew he could invent enough bullshit about wizards and zombies and fucking spells to convince the former baseball-coach that he was doing alright, and best not bother him too much.

"Jeez, son," Gourd began after they all sat down on those little blue beds with disposable sanitation sheets crumpling noisily atop them. He looked entirely depressing. "I don't think there's a spell we can cast to get you out of this cave."

Henry smiled, affecting as much sincerity as he could. The look on his father's face in response to Gourd's sage metaphor made it quite hard not to laugh.

Dunks stood up, making Henry wonder why he'd sat down in the first place, and said, "Listen Henry, I'm going to give it to you straight. Young man, I'm terribly afraid that after the actions, err, the *discovery*, of uh...Well, I'll just get right to it then. After the events which transpired just this morning, with you and Jerry, err, Mr. *Welsh* here, involving you and your car, and various, what shall we call them, *substances*, well and per the student handbook, the rules, we might have given you a suspension, you see. But after a thorough investigation of everything confiscated by Mr. Welsh, we have deduced that there is no other logical explanation than that you had the intent to distribute these, uh, substances— presumably to members of the St. Dominic's student body. And that, young man, simply cannot fly. We are left with no other choice but to expel you, immediately. And as for your remaining two exams..."

Henry wondered how immediately Dunks meant by "immediately." Could he just stand up and leave? Was his mother crying? She wasn't. He wondered if his parents would ever see the stash that Welsh had grabbed. If they'd see that Henry had been stealing his little brother Pete's Adderall bottles, and probably the Adderall too. And that they were wrong in accusing Pete of selling his prescription drugs to his friends, after the prescriptions ran out too soon. And that maybe they shouldn't have sent Pete to that "Get Back on the Right Path!" sort of summer camp thing last year.

Dunks was speaking, and Henry truly wasn't listening. Or perhaps, he truly wasn't hearing. He watched the man's mouth move, watched the spittle fly out every so often, but heard nothing.

His Mom asked a question about something, and smiled, and looked reassured, and Dunks handed her some pre-made packet. Henry wondered if they had a pile of these expulsion packets lying around somewhere, if they were thicker or lighter than suspension packets.

His dad's phone alarm went off. Henry heard that, for sure. It was the same sound as his morning alarm.

"Sorry, gentlemen, if you'll excuse me, where is the nearest bathroom?" his Dad said. It was time for his pills, which meant it was noon. Which meant everybody had already left to go to the catered reception in the AC. Which meant that if they hurried all of this up, Henry could get out of there without anyone seeing him.

The nurses were listening to "Good Riddance" by Green Day from the little speakers in their little office as Henry and his parents and his advisor and the Dean of Students and the Head of School all migrated together from the back room they'd been stationed in to the waiting room. Some freshman girl Henry half-recognized was sitting down on the couch.

"Well, son, I'm sorry it had to come to this. Best of luck," from Welsh.

"You may collect your things from your lockers at a later date, which we can arrange with your parents," from Dunks.

"You know, kiddo," from Gourd, with an honest-to-god tear, "sometimes you've just got to saddle back up after you've been hit. There are new dungeons to explore. Go get 'em, kid."

His parents didn't say anything, which Henry appreciated, as they walked to the parking lot. There, their paths diverged.

"Where are you going?" Henry asked.

"Our car's parked over here," his mother replied. "We'll meet you at the house?"

When he got to his car, Henry considered taking everything left and hiding it somewhere on campus. Over his right shoulder, however, were Welsh and Dunks, chatting to each other but looking straight at him. Presumably seeing him off.

He always figured he'd be sitting shotgun on the drive home, if he ever got expelled. It was inexplicably crueler that he had to drive alone, making all the stoplights and turns and fields and shops he'd seen every day on his drive home from school somewhat saccharine and real.

He imagined that a lot of people would be feeling that way today, leaving St. Dominic's campus for the last time. Some would be driving themselves, but most would be crammed into cars with their families and everything they'd had in their dorm rooms. Off to whatever family luncheon or family party they were off to, before the evening's real festivities. And they, too, would be looking out the window, on their own paths back home.

He thought of a college essay question he'd been just casually looking over the other day. "*Where do you see yourself in 100 years? (500 words)*" The school was either optimistic about life expectancies in the future, or the poor Admissions sap just fucked up the prompt by one zero.

He got stopped by a red at a light he usually didn't get stopped at. Welsh was a real fucking idiot for not seeing the Juul that was right there in Henry's pocket, its outline creased in his tight pants. He took a couple of rips and sighed. No cars behind him, no cars in front. No cars crossing. No pedestrian traffic either.

The light switched back green, but Henry didn't move. He just sat there and watched the nothing all around him.

///*Yes, when Henry was in Kindergarten he had combined the two naughtiest words he knew into the miraculous 'fuckcunt,' a verbal epiphany he then loudly and emphatically accused his pediatrician of being after administering a shot.*///

# THE SNOW DAY. 7:57 PM.

———

Most of the guys that would care had caught wind of Mark's bad trip, and were popping in to check in on him.

Todd was the first. He talked about his "date" with Sarah, talked about the food, the drinks. Todd's fake ID had worked at the restaurant, so he was feeling happy. With Frank in the room, Todd really made a point to use the word "date" as many times as he could. Although it obviously wasn't *really* a date, Todd just wanted to get to know Sarah. He mentioned that part to Mark as an aside, awkwardly leaning over to whisper that he was just fucking with Frank.

Todd and Frank had an interesting relationship, Mark gathered. Neither one really understood the other, but they were past the point of wondering why they hung out.

Todd clearly wanted to know what Mark's experience had been like tripping hard on shrooms, but he never asked.

Chris came in right as Todd was leaving. Chris didn't really know what to say, so instead of talking to Mark he chatted with Birdie and Frank. He kept glancing at Mark, though. After about ten minutes, Chris left to go do homework.

Birdie and Frank had set themselves up as watchdogs over Mark, but they were both getting tired and probably had better shit to do. Despite Mark telling them repeatedly that he was fine, they begrudgingly stood guard.

The name *Grace* never came up.

Apparently the story with Birdie was that he had to cancel on his leg of the double date, and that Carissa took it well. Birdie was hung up with guilt about the whole ordeal, which transitively made Mark feel pretty shitty.

The bad trip never really ended. Mark just woke up suddenly, when the Valium kicked in. The abruptness of it left Mark with the strangest kind of hangover he'd ever felt. There wasn't a clean break that he could remember, nor a gradient of change experienced. There was simply the Before, the memories of which lingered abstractly in his mind, and the After, which was the abrupt re-immersion into the normal.

The day felt like it had lasted four years.

Mark was tired, but couldn't imagine sleeping. In fact, he made a point to blink as quickly as he could whenever his eyes got dry. The thought of being alone in darkness with nothing but his memories terrified him. What if it happened again?

*///Of course, it would happen again. It was always happening, and always had been. He carried with him only his memories, despite his intentions. Or perhaps, in spite of his intentions.///*

# TUESDAY, DECEMBER 18TH, 2018. 2:51 PM.

———

Todd banged his head against the wall.

He'd fucked up his English exam that morning. He had to write an essay on—

He banged his head against the wall again.

He'd thought a couple of beers in the morning would loosen him up, get the creative juices—

*Bang.*

And afterwards, after their final winter exams, he and Birdie had plans to have a couple of celebratory—

*Bang.*

And then Birdie's parents were on their way to pick him up for winter break so Todd, well, he had to start packing, because his own parentals were coming to pick *him* up soon enough. After Birdie had left, Todd went back to his room to have a couple of more so conciliatory—

*Bang.*

And then he'd gotten the text from his parents that they'd be there in thirty minutes, and he realized he had to start packing but it was hard to—

*Bang.*

And instead of packing Todd thought he'd just have one more—

*Bang.*

The freshman Miles came into his room, maybe without knocking first. There was a pile of empty beer cans on the floor.

"Yo, what's going on, Todd? Ben and I thought you were like hammering something into your wall."

"Please don't tell Birdie," Todd said.

Miles helped him pack up his stuff into the suitcase under his bed. Underwear, socks, two pairs of shoes, four pairs of khakis, eight shirts, two quarter-zips, one winter coat.

Todd remembered to pack his pocket pussy, which he did while Miles wasn't looking. He also decided to put on his beanie rather than pack it, to cover any formulating discoloration on his forehead from his parents.

"I'm sorry, man," Todd said. Neither of them had mentioned the cans on the floor.

"Don't sweat it, dude," said Miles, standing by the door.

"It's all just really hard."

"Is it that much harder than freshman year?"

Todd didn't reply. He was getting a call from his Mom, which meant his parents were either five minutes away or already on campus. He needed water. Miles had slipped out the door.

In the car ride home Todd didn't say much. Just, as soberly as he could manage, "I think I did alright," and, "I'm just super tired."

///His dad preferred to take the backroads. Todd looked out the window at the naked trees and the thin layer of frozen snow, the ponds and farms he'd passed by countless times on drives to and from St. D's. The bright blue sky speckled with hints of clouds, the last cyclists and the first marathon trainees. The mom-and-pop shops and the stop signs and the front-yard picket signs promoting local politicians. The yellow-brown fields and white churches. The history of the land, the thick of it. The everything beyond sight, beyond comprehension. The sentimental stone found on a family hike, age six. The laughter *after dark, warmed inside from the threat of snowfall. The cycles of seasons. The recursive conversations.*

*Their breaths in the cold, dissipating faster than they could exhale again.///*

# THE FIRST DAY OF SCHOOL. 10:59 PM.

———

"Hey Mark?"

"Yeah?"

"Are you awake?"

"Dude, we turned the lights off like two seconds ago."

"Can you hear me alright from down here?"

"Are you in a tunnel?"

"Very funny."

"What's up?"

"Not much. You?"

"Whaddaya think of the freshmen?"

"Good group of guys, from what I can tell. Todd'll have some
 fun with them."

"Toddle. What a stupid fucking name."

"Right?"

"It's kinda hot in here."

"Yeah."

"Hey Birdie?"

"Yeah?"

"Isn't Grace looking real good these days?"

"Absolute snipe, my guy."

"Thanks."

"You know I really missed these late night conversations."

"You mean over the summer?"

"I mean, like, yeah."

"I know what you mean."

"It's like, nice, you know. To talk to someone without actually seeing them."

"How's that any different from just talking over the phone?"

"Mark, you can be a real imbecile when you want to be."

"I always want to be."

"Alright. Top three hottest girls in the grade. Who ya got?"

"This again?"

"This again. It's been a long summer."

"You're a horny bastard, you know that?"

"Not all of us have suddenly-hot girlfriends."

"Yes, but all of us could suddenly *have* hot girlfriends."

"You're dodging the question."

"Grace, Grace, aaaaand Grace."

"You know, you don't have to be like that. What am I gonna do, tell her?"

"Why don't you answer then first, Mr. Birdmeister."

"Well the thing is I don't know."

"You wanna say Grace don't you? At least top three?"

"Shut up, fuck you. Never mind then."

"Dude, you know what I was thinking about the other day?"

"What's that?"

"Remember that time you and Todd superglued Dr. Stein's keyhole?"

"Of course, pinnacle of our pranks."

"Only it wasn't just a prank, was it?"

"You might say there was a tactical layer to it. Toddster and I had a first-block chem test that morning which neither of us felt particularly good about."

"So instead of studying…"

"So instead of studying we made sure Dr. Stein wouldn't be able to get into her classroom."

"And the test got moved?"

"The test got moved, class got cancelled, maintenance guys got called—the whole shebang."

"That's, like, a glitch in the matrix, Birdie. Shit like that isn't supposed to work to the tee."

"But it did."

"But it did."

"You know what else is like a glitch in the matrix? Condensation."

"How's that?"

"You put water in a glass, and then you look away, and all of a sudden the water is outside the glass."

"Right."

"And we all just take it for granted, like, *oh there's a word for that so it's definitely not a fucking glitch.*"

"I feel like science can explain that."

"I told you I was no good at chemistry."

"Is that even chemistry?"

"You and Grace have chemistry."

"Not really."

"Yeah that was a joke."

"I don't know if you could hear my sigh from down there."

"When are you gonna break up with her?"

"I don't think I can."

"Of course you can. Unless it's a whole now-she's-hot sorta thing."

"Can we drop it?"

"I dunno man, if you split with her now chicks are gonna see you as someone who gets with hot chicks, and so the girls will come lining up."

"I don't think it's that easy, young sparrow."

"It's 'young grasshopper.'"

"I dunno. Birdie, sparrow. I thought it worked."

"Alright new question, master Mark. What the fuck kinda shit do you wanna get up to this year?"

"See that's the way I wish my advisor would ask me, instead of *list three goals for the year*."

"Right?"

"Right. I dunno man, I wanna get up to some shit."

"Like what?"

"I don't know."

"I feel you."

"What's there to do?"

"What's there *not* to do?"

"Who's on first?"

"Very funny."

"You know, Birdo, you could laugh sometimes, rather than just declare things as being funny."

"Hey Mark?"

"Yeah?"

"Nothing."

"Come on."

"Do you think you're going to change?"

"Bro, miss me with that shit."

"No, come on. Do you think you're gonna change?"

"When?"

"I'm asking you."

"With any luck."

"You know what my name means?"

"Small mammal that can fly?"

"Birds are *reptiles*, dumbass. I meant my last name."

"Fayter?"

"Fayter. It means *doer* or *maker.*"

"What do you intend to do or make?"

"I don't know. I don't think anything, really."

"That's deep."

"Hey Mark?"

"Still awake."

"Wanna hear something scary?"

"Boo?"

"You're—*we're* going to be thirty-five someday."

"With any luck."

"Is that so?"

"I don't know. Is this like some sort of hold-on-to-your-youth-while-it-lasts sorta thing?"

"Is what that sort of thing?"

"This."

"I don't think so. Besides, how can I hold onto my youth?"

"Crossfit. Sex. Botox, eventually. Are birds really reptiles?"

"Who do you think will get married first?"

"You."

"No way."

"Hey Birdie?"

"*My how the turn tables.* What's up?"

"You sound like Grace."

"How's that?"

"All she does is, like, quote *The Office*."

"It's a good show."

"But, like, basing your whole personality off of a show?"

"Hey, doesn't she like *Friends* too?"

"Fuck you."

"What's up?"

"I think I have a crush on Carissa Moraine."

"Don't be so predictable, Mark."

"I also think I'm addicted to porn."

"Why wouldn't you be?"

"Hey, Birdie."

"Still listening."

"How do you remember the past?"

"What kind of porn?"

"I don't really like anything with a dick in it."

"You must hate Grace then."

"Very funny."

"A laugh would've been nice, by your own standards. I remember the past...like what past?"

"Like recent past, like the past couple of years."

"I think it's funny to think about it."

"How so?"

"Like, take that story of me and Toodles fucking with Stein's keyhole. You know what else happened that day?"

"What?"

"Todd caught a touchdown pass."

"No shit?"

"I remember because while Todd was catching his touchdown pass, I was off with Maury getting high in the woods."

"Is that so?"

"And we made plans to smoke during the time I got off from Stein's cancelled class. And I know Todd caught that touchdown that day because when Maury and I were walking back everyone was yelling 'Todd Down!' and I was so high I kept looking at the ground, expecting to see Todd materialize beneath me."

"What's the point?"

"The point is I remember all three, or I guess like two, of those memories, but I don't remember when they happened."

"But it sounds like you do."

"Okay, yeah, like now that I actually have to sit and think about it."

"You're sitting?"

"Well I'm lying."

"What other connections do you think you could make if you sat down to think about it?"

"That's the best part. I think if I really sat down, I could remember everything."

"That'd take some time. You'd have to free up your schedule. That'd take a lot of superglue."

"Exactly. Who has time to remember everything?"

"Isn't it funny, what we end up remembering."

"And what we can be reminded of."

"Do you think they're the same? Like, is actively being able to recollect something on your own the same as being able to recollect it when you're reminded?"

"Well whose job is it to remind you to remember?"

"Hey Birdie?"

*///...you might miss it.///*

# ACKNOWLEDGMENTS

———

I wouldn't have been able to write this book were it not for the support of friends, family, and countless others. Among them are Aidan Conway, Alex Scott, Alexis Bradley, Amy and Rufus Rumrill, Aurelie Chuong, Barbara O'Hara, Brian Black, Brian and Sumiko Courtney, Brian Ely, Bruce Courtney, Charlie Abrams, Chris Lemley, Chris Scalia, Colton Scrudder, Cooper Buch, Corey Hutson, Cristin Allen, Daniel Kerfoot, Danielle Darasz, Deborah Han, Doug and Nancy Cole, Doug Eckelkamp, Earl and Joanne Cate, Eric Koester, Eric Silberstein, Ezra Muratoglu, Giao Phan, Greg Linton, Griffin McCombs, Hannah Nichols, Harrison Clark, Harry Craig, Jessie Cahill, Julie Ghostlaw, Kamron Landry, Kevin McGrath, Kimberly LaValle, Kirsten Johnson and Amy Blackburn, Laura Boynton, Linda Wolf, Pete DiNatale, Rachel Thomas, Robbie Winthrop, Sam Joseph, Scott and Sue Courtney, Scott Enos, Seamus Masterson, Susan Brown, Teddy Matel, Vincent Fernald, Yumi Sakaguchi, and Zachary Curtis

# ACKNOWLEDGMENTS

CPSIA information can be obtained
at www.ICGtesting.com
Printed in the USA
FSHW020402151220
76882FS